S0-BOW-712

STRATEGIC
BIBLICAL
COUNSELING

1,48
32
(480)

STRATEGIC BIBLICAL COUNSELING

A model for
pastors and lay
counselors

Dr. H Greg Burts

Pleasant W rd

© 2004 by Dr. H. Greg Burts. All rights reserved

Packaged by Pleasant Word, PO Box 428, Enumclaw, WA 98022. The views expressed or implied in this work do not necessarily reflect those of Pleasant Word. The author(s) is ultimately responsible for the design, content and editorial accuracy of this work.

No part of this publication may be reproduced, stored in a retrieval system or transmitted in any way by any means—electronic, mechanical, photocopy, recording or otherwise—without the prior permission of the copyright holder, except as provided by USA copyright law.

All Scriptures are taken from the New American Standard Bible, © 1960, 1963, 1968, 1971, 1972, 1973, 1975, 1977 by The Lockman Foundation. Used by permission.

ISBN 1-4141-0344-1
Library of Congress Catalog Card Number: 2004099627

Table of Contents

Preface

In 1981, after ten years of *prodigal* living, I found myself in my own self-imposed pig pen. I could no longer deny the emptiness. There was no purpose; I had no reason to live. The world of fun and excitement I had sought was meaningless. In the words of Job: "They conceive mischief, and bring forth vanity" (Job 15:35).

Like the prodigal, however, I "came to his [my] senses" (Luke 15:17) and began my journey home. Recommitted to my spiritual roots, my lifestyle of partying, clubs and drugs began to change. And a new lifestyle of *letting go* and *saying no* replaced the old lifestyle of *if it feels good, do it*!

However, the real issue was not just changing my behaviors and associations. That was all external, and I had grown up playing that game. I was looking for something internal. The reality of being what-the-Bible-calls a *new creature* was something that had always eluded me in my years of growing up in the church. And so in pursuit of genuine *mind renewal* I immersed myself in the Scriptures. Each day I awoke 30 minutes before my normal time to read the Bible and pray. Then I rearranged my work schedule so that on my way to work, I could listen to radio Bible teachers like Chuck Swindoll, Charles Stanley, Jack Hayford and John MacArthur. I ordered their tapes and studied at home. Before long, I was spending more time studying the Bible and listening to tapes than watching TV. And ultimately I gave that away so I would not be tempted to waste my time.

I began going to church again. I joined a single's fellowship. I taught children's Sunday school. I started a Bible study at work. By the end of that first year, I was discipling other men. I discovered I had an interest in helping, teaching and encouraging other believers; I was learning to use the Bible to stimulate and strengthen others' walk. I began to pursue more opportunities to share the things I had learned. Then it happened: the Lord put an idea in my mind—to be a Biblical counselor.

One day in 1983 I had lunch with an older, wiser brother in Christ; I shared my idea about Biblical counseling. He told me about a woman who had a Biblical counseling ministry in Palo Alto. Her name was Altha Thompson. I called and made an appointment with her. I was eager to know how Altha had come to know about Biblical counseling. And I was delighted to meet a like-minded person with whom I could share my vision for a Biblical counseling ministry.

The week before I met Altha, I ran into someone who was acquainted with her. He said to me, "You'd better read Charles Solomon's book *Handbook to Happiness* so you will understand what Altha is talking about. It explains what it means to be a 'new creation.'" When I heard the word *new creation*, I knew that God was behind this divine appointment with Altha. That weekend, I read Charles Solomon's book. And for the first time in my life I understood what the apostle Paul meant when he said,

Therefore, if any man is in Christ, he is a new creature; the old things have passed away; behold, all things have become new .

(2 Corinthians 5:17)

The revelation of this truth to me, and its effect on my thinking and subsequent behavior, is the basis of my framework for Biblical counseling.

Now let me share a word about my wife Altha.

In 1978, Altha recognized her *calling* from the Lord to minister to hurting people. Raised in an abusive home, she became a ward of the court, followed by years of being raised in foster homes. Growing up in this dysfunctional world, Altha suffered the consequences of these historical influences until, at the age of 27, she was brought into the kingdom of God and began to discover the reality of being a child of God's family. [You can read about Altha's journey in her book *Come Up Higher*, published by Pleasant Word, 2005.]

In obedience to the Lord's call, Altha traveled from California to Denver, Colorado where she interned at Grace Fellowship Institute, learning the basics of Biblical counseling. Upon her return, Altha began counseling out of her apartment in Mountain View. Soon she was receiving so many referrals, she needed an office. God confirmed her "call" by the gift of office space by a Christian chiropractor in downtown Los Altos. Barely bigger than a walk-in closet, the office was outfitted and adorned by the gifts and donations of those who shared Altha's vision to establish a ministry of Biblical counseling. Over the next several years, her ministry developed and grew in reputation as many hurting persons experienced the restorative power of God's Word and the wholeness that God provides to His beloved children.

And so it was that God led me to Altha's office in March 1983. Within months of our first meeting, Altha and I knew God was calling us not only to ministry but to marriage. We married in June the following year. I quit my employment in San Francisco to join Altha in the ministry of Biblical counseling. Having no training, I had many questions about methods and the process of helping people to change. I had questions about why people do the things they do. I was eager to understand the "issues." Subsequently, I applied to Azusa Pacific University's extension program (in the Bay Area) to earn a Masters of Arts degree in Marriage, Family and Child Counseling. There were so many psychological models for diagnosing and treating one's clients, I became increasingly confused as I attempted to find my way through the maze of theories while maintaining my commitment to Biblical counseling. But the educational experience only confirmed my belief that the path to real change was not psychological—it was spiritual. And the road map was not a college textbook—it was the Bible.

Although I attended a Christian university, it became clear to me that this post-graduate counseling program was more focused on meeting the State's licensure requirements than on making effective Christian counselors. And as I had more contact with the community of Christian counselors, both through the university and through my own networking, it became apparent that very few, if any, of these Christian therapists had a working definition of Christian counseling. I was therefore challenged to develop my own clear definition of Christian counseling. Eventually, I began to use the term "Biblical counseling" because it more clearly distinguished Christian counseling from secular therapy.

After graduating in 1987, I began to write and develop the Biblical counseling model presented in this book. Since then, the material has undergone many revisions and has been taught in dozens of churches in the States and overseas.

In 1993 the Lord called me to pastor a church in Sunnyvale, California. During that time, I grew personally as I taught and pastored a small group of dear brothers and sisters in the Lord. Then in 1998, after a 5-year hiatus from Biblical counseling, the Lord renewed my vision to establish a Biblical counseling ministry. Accordingly, I founded the Center for Biblical Counseling to teach and train others. With that in mind, I decided to get a Ph.D. in psychology so that I would have a recognizable academic and professional platform from which to speak to pastors and Christian counselors. While this training has given me a broader view of the *science* of psychology, diagnostically and therapeutically, I continue to assert: I am not a psychologist; I am a Biblical counselor.

Greg Burts

Introduction

THE NEED FOR BIBLICAL COUNSELOR TRAINING

Scenario:

Across from Pastor John's desk sat Mary and Mark, a couple who had come in to see him because they were having marital problems. Mary had recently discovered Mark accessing pornography websites on his computer. She was devastated not only because it was so contrary to their values but also because it had affected the trust level in their relationship. And as is also common, it caused Mary to feel undervalued by her husband. As Mary tearfully expressed her pain and Mark painfully explained how he had come to this point of sexual addiction, Pastor John was silently praying: "Lord, help me, because I don't know where to begin." He would have preferred to send Mary and Mark to a competent Christian therapist, but he knew they did not have the money to pay for "professional" help. Pastor John felt so inadequate and unequipped to help his parishioners, as he listened and waited to respond, he said: "Lord, help me!"

The Baby Boomer generation has been witness to a paradigm shift to postmodern relativism—rejecting absolute, objective truth. Two thousand years of Judeo Christian social structure and moral values have been abandoned. Church attendance in the United States has reached an all-time low. Not surprisingly, a psychologically disturbed generation has emerged. And adding to this, because of increased mobilization, individuals have moved away from the families and communities that supported their beliefs and values. They are without a moral anchor (*Where there is no guidance the people fall*, Proverbs 10:14).

For centuries, moral values, ethics and lifestyle were dictated by religious beliefs. Dating back to the time of Moses, mentoring, advising, and counseling have been a natural function of corporate spiritual life. In the New Testament, believers carried out the commands to *admonish one another* (Romans 15:14), *exhort one another daily* (Hebrews 3:13), *encourage . . . and build up one another* (1 Thessalonians 5:11), *confess . . . sins to one another, pray for one another, in order to be healed* (James 5:16), and *stimulate one another to love and good deeds* (Hebrews 10:24).

Christians today are seeking professional psychological services in increasing numbers. Professional Christian counseling has become very marketable. Mainline denominations now refer their members to Christian therapists, Christian counseling clinics, and seminars on various psychological subjects (from a Christian worldview, of course). However, paying $100 an hour or more for counseling is prohibitive for too many people. Thus, hurting people (Christians and non-Christians alike) are looking to the church for their counseling needs. While most pastors want to meet this increased demand, they are feeling overwhelmed.

There are legitimate issues that make pastoral counseling problematic. Pastors are frustrated by the added demands on their time. Pastors are discouraged by their lack of expertise—acknowledging that their theological training prepared them for their pulpit responsibility, but not for counseling duties. What is a pastor to do?

Many churches have found the solution is to establish lay counseling ministries, where mature, gifted persons within the church are able to do this work of pastoral care. Identifying, training, and empowering these people can be difficult, but the rewards are well worth the effort. Lay counseling ministries can provide a valuable service to those who need it; they provide a ministry opportunity for mature believers to use their gifts; and they free the pastor's time and energy for other pastoral duties.

However, I must warn the reader that the task of identifying training resources can be daunting. Many lay counselor training programs rely on therapeutic principles and practices. These programs train lay counselors to be little more than "pseudo-therapists." Churches need a counselor training program that provides both a framework and a therapeutic approach that draws from the Bible—not from psychology. A recent internet search reveals very few books have been written in the last 30 years on the subject of Biblical counseling, and as of this writing, no book has been written on the subject in the last 10 years.

I must also acknowledge that many pastors I have spoken with are afraid to use lay counselors in their churches: they are afraid of malpractice liability. These fears are not exactly unwarranted. There have been lawsuits. But if a church "lay" counseling ministry clearly distinguishes itself from secular therapy, the counselors—and therefore local churches—are not liable to malpractice. As long as a church clearly distinguishes that its lay counselors are operating in a pastoral role—an extension of a church's pastoral care—there can be no basis for malpractice. Why?

The courts have uniformly rejected claims of counseling malpractice brought against pastors—because courts have found that in order to assess whether a pastor has breached his duty of care to the person being counseled, the court would need to evaluate the church's religious beliefs and how well the pastor carried out his pastoral responsibilities. Obviously, courts view this as excessive entanglement of government with religion and a violation of the First Amendment to the United States Constitution. Therefore, courts have rejected malpractice suits brought against churches.

Lay Biblical counseling ministries actually have some advantages over the professional counseling centers outside the church. First, working in tandem with the pastor, they extend the effectiveness of the pastors' shepherding responsibilities. Second, they advance the objectives of the pastor as they promote spiritual growth, helping counselees to apply the Word of God to issues. And third, Biblical counselors working within the local church can avail themselves of church resources—care groups, Bible studies, prayer groups, men's and women's fellowships, discipleships, mentoring programs, and recovery ministries.

For 2000 years, local churches have been the recognized community resources for counsel and advice. Modern day Christian psychotherapy is a replacement for what-used-to-be a pastoral function of caring for souls. Increasingly, the Christian psychology movement is marginalizing pastors and church leaders who are no longer being taken seriously with respect to counseling. Secular psychology has slipped in through the back door of the church; it is chipping away at the foundation of absolute truth. Even many Christian psychologists have lost their bearings. It is time to return the ministry of pastoral care and counseling to the church. However, pastors and church counselors need a model of Biblical counseling that is simple, sound, and strategic—one that will instruct mature Christian leaders how to counsel their weaker brothers and sisters in Christ effectively.

Pastors and church leaders, as you set your strategy for your church's counseling ministry, remember the primary means of spiritual growth: the straightforward, Christ-centered proclamation of the unadulterated Word of God. If you trade the Word for psychological insights, you will not only find yourself with no effective means to empower the people you counsel, but you will also find yourself at cross purposes with the Lord Himself. Do not be intimidated by psychologists. If you do, you will be operating from fear, not power. Do not forget the promise of sufficiency in Paul's letter to the Ephesians: *[God is] able to do exceeding abundantly above all that we ask or think, according to the power that works in us* (3:20).

OVERVIEW OF THE BOOK

This purpose of this book is to provide 1) a framework for Biblical counseling and 2) a strategy for applying that framework to individual needs. The first two chapters of this book answer two basic questions: What is Biblical counseling? and What is a Biblical counselor? Unfortunately, there is no consensus among Christian psychologists and therapists, pastors, and church leaders as to what "Christian" counseling is. These chapters present a Scriptural basis for Biblical counseling.

Chapters three through nine build the doctrinal framework for Biblical counseling. These chapters address the doctrines of God, Christ, Holy Spirit, man, sin, sanctification, and Christian living. My purpose in presenting these "doctrinal" themes in these brief chapters is to show the link between sound teaching and effective counseling. Sound doctrine is the basis for Strategic Biblical Counseling. These doctrines provide us answers to our counselee's questions: Why did God make me this way? Can I change? Why is it such a struggle to live the Christian life? How can I change? Without a good knowledge of these doctrines, the Biblical counselor will not be able to answer such questions with confidence, thus giving hope to and increasing the faith of his counselee.

Lest anyone should accuse me of presumption in trying to address such great doctrinal themes in such brevity, let me assure you I agree it would be. Or I would be very naïve if I thought I could do so. This book is written for those who already know these doctrines, but may not know how to integrate them with a practical application in counseling settings. I confess I was particularly frustrated by the daunting task of expositing Romans 6 in the chapter called "Can I Change?" (chapter 6), and the various scriptures in the chapter called "Why is it Such a Struggle?" (chapter 7). For a wonderful exposition of these themes, I recommend Martin Lloyd Jones' expositional series on the book of Romans, particularly the volumes on Romans 6 and 7. For a more practical approach to these themes, I recommend the classic *The Normal Christian Life* by Watchman Nee and *Birthright* by David Needham. Other authors I have gleaned from are too numerous to mention. Word studies that are presented in this book are taken from *The Complete Word Study New Testament [and Old Testament]*, compiled and edited by Spiros Zodhiates, AMG Publishers, 1992. These have been an excellent resource for finding the nuggets that open up the Scriptures in a practical way.

Having laid the foundation for Biblical counseling, chapter ten provides the reader with a strategic treatment plan to address his counselee's issues. This strategic treatment plan instructs the counselor in how to conduct a session, diagnose the problem, set goals, monitor progress, and assign homework.

The last two chapters illustrate how to set up and execute a counseling session based on the framework and the strategic treatment plan presented in the preceding chapters. Specifically, the counselor learns how to organize a treatment plan for a counselee whose presenting problem is anger or depression. Each of these chapters is illustrated by a full counseling scenario that will walk the reader through the treatment steps.

CHAPTER ONE

What is Biblical Counseling?

The question of what **is**—and what **is not**—"Christian" in counseling has become the bane of the Western evangelical church in our time. The debate has resulted in many articles and books written by well-meaning Christian psychologists and pastors attempting to reconcile or integrate models of psychology with Christian principles. While it is my strong desire to avoid that dispute in this book, I am persuaded to make some comparisons in order to clarify my position for the reader.

Let me begin with this reference point. All models of psychological counseling are based on a *theoretical framework*. A theory can be defined as a speculation about how things are organized, based on observations. These observations are formalized into a theory through scientific studies of human behavior.

The Bible also provides a *framework* for counseling. This framework, however, is not based on speculations or observations. Rather, it is based on an **absolute** view of humanity, moral values, and character. These Biblically based absolutes are given in the form of commandments, laws, statutes, precepts, and exhortations.

The *framework* for psychological counseling has been greatly affected by postmodernism, defining humans as free and autonomous individuals. Postmodern thought is a rejection of absolute, objective truth in favor of relativism. Therefore, any counseling theory that is based on observing human behaviors is relative "truth"—not absolute truth. If the *framework* from which the counselor works is flawed, his conclusions will be wrong.

The most powerful weapon given to the Church, and to the Biblical counselor, is spiritual truth. The only source for absolute truth is the Bible. It is the believer's plumb line and his compass. And the Bible is the basis for defining humanity and determining morality. It is the believer's *framework*. Whatever theories social scientists may deduce from their observations, in the end it is God's view of man that matters. And God's view of man is delineated in the Bible, a *framework* not only adequate to address his issues, but superior to any other (2 Timothy 3:16–17).

BIBLICAL COUNSELING MEANS USING GOD'S WORD

The writer of Hebrews declares the power of the Word of God when he says: "[it] is living and active and sharper than a two-edge sword . . ." (Hebrews 4:12). The absolute *authority* of Scripture and the *power* of the Word are the Biblical counselor's guarantee of success. The Biblical counselor actually *uses* the Scriptures in counseling, believing that the "words" give life. *For this reason we also constantly thank God that when you received the word of God which you heard from us, you accepted it not as the word of men, but for what it really is, the word of God which also performs its work in you who believe* (1 Thessalonians 2:13). To effectively *use* Scripture in counseling, the Biblical counselor must *know* the Scriptures so that the Holy Spirit can bring them to mind (John 16:13).

Biblical Counseling is Spiritual Communication

Counseling works optimally when *communication* between the counselor and counselee is clear, logical, reasonable, and comprehensible. For this reason, Biblical counselors rely on **spirit-to-spirit** communication, knowing that *spiritual language* is the highest form of communication (John 6:63). Through the Biblical counselor, the Holy Spirit communicates truth to the counselee. Before the counselee ever comes to his first counseling session, the Holy Spirit is already working in him to reveal the truth he needs to know. Therefore, Biblical counselors prayerfully yield control of each counseling session, knowing that the Holy Spirit is the Communicator. They wait on the Holy Spirit to manifest Himself in wisdom, discernment, correction, encouragement, and instruction. Counselor and counselee recognize that the agenda for each session emanates from the Holy Spirit.

The Holy Spirit was given to testify of Jesus (John 15:26; 16:14). The Holy Spirit will not anoint counseling that does not draw men to Jesus (John 16:13). Drawing men closer to Jesus is *not* a byproduct of counseling. Rather, it is the essence of Biblical counseling (John 12:32).

The Holy Spirit was given to teach and instruct the believer and reveal truth (John 16:13). He reveals God to the human spirit (1 Corinthians 2:13). He renews the minds (Romans 8:6). But this is not merely a mental experience, but one whereby He supernaturally enables the believer to comprehend spiritual truth.

The Holy Spirit was given to sanctify the believer (James 4:5), indwelling the believer (1 Corinthians 6:19; Romans 8:9). The Holy Spirit works in the counselee to bring about a change (Romans 8:13). He exposes sin and brings the believer to repentance (John 16:8–11). He bears fruit in the counselee's life (Galatians 5:16, 18, 22–26).

The Biblical counselor's role is to discern how the Holy Spirit is working in the counselee's life. He views himself as a facilitator of the Holy Spirit's work, e.g., repentance, confession, obedience.

BIBLICAL COUNSELING IS CHRIST-CENTERED, NOT ISSUE-CENTERED

Secular psychological counseling presents a man-centered approach to life. It focuses on his issues. Significantly, when Adam and Eve sinned, they became immediately aware of themselves. For the first time, they were self-conscious—they focused on their nakedness (Genesis 3:7). Symbolically, they became *issue-centered*. They began looking at their problem trying to fix it. When they could not cover up their *issue*, they tried to hide it. God's immediate solution to their problem was to kill an animal and provide a covering for them. This is a foreshadowing of the Lamb of God. The only answer to a believer's "issues" is the sacrificial work of Jesus Christ, that is, His covering or atonement for sin(s)—sin issues.

Rather than being *issue-centered*, Biblical counseling is *Christ-centered*. The Biblical counselor leads the counselee to Christ, imparting a vision for Christ-centered living. Instead of focusing on the sin issue, the Biblical counselor focuses the counselee on Jesus (Hebrews 12:2). The Bible says we become slaves to the things we pay attention to (Romans 6:16). As long as counselees are paying attention to their issues, they continue in bondage to them.

One of the greatest deceptions in the area of counseling is that pastors and church leaders must be experts on the issues. A cottage industry of "issue" seminars has grown in the last few decades. While there is merit in understanding the issues, the pastor and Biblical counselor must be careful not to become issue-oriented. In the fourth chapter of Ephesians Paul states it most succinctly:1) put off the old self (the issues), 2) be renewed in the spirit of your mind, and 3) put on the new self. Understanding issues is necessary in order to know what to *put off* (repent of), but the focus of Biblical counseling *is renewed thinking* and *obedience from a renewed heart* (Romans 6:17; 12:2). Biblical counselors know that a person must be changed from the *inside-out*.

In the Old Testament, the prophets were given to Israel to keep the people focused on God and His commandments and to bring correction to the people whenever they drifted from God's teachings. Like Old Testament prophets, Biblical counselors direct their counselees back to Christ. While the goal of counseling may be for the counselee to feel, function, or behave better, these will never be truly attained without an approach that is *Christ-centered.*

BIBLICAL COUNSELING IS NOT "NATURAL"

In the New Testament, three different Greek words are translated *life*. *Bios* refers to physical, biological life. *Psuche* refers to soul life (mind, emotions, and will). *Pneuma* refers to spiritual life. Man is created body, soul, and spirit. The Greek word for the *human spirit* is *pneuma.*

In the second chapter of his first letter to the Corinthians, Paul separates humanity into two categories: 1) *natural* man and 2) *spiritual* man. Significantly, the word for *natural man* is *psuchikos:* which could be translated "soulical." The parallel word for *spiritual man* is *pneumatikos.* Since the Word of God is spiritual, only a spiritual man can comprehend it. Paul prays for the Ephesians that the "eyes of [their] heart" might be opened, and for "strengthening" in their "inner man" (1:18; 3:16). The "eyes of the heart" and the "inner man" refer to the deepest part of a person: the SPIRIT of a man. In Ephesians, Paul prays: *be renewed in the spirit of your mind.* The spirit of the mind means the innermost part. The spirit is the part of man that connects him to GOD, who is *Spirit* (John 4:24). Paul says *the natural man cannot understand the things of God, for they are spiritually appraised [evaluated, discerned], but the spiritual man appraises [evaluates, discerns] all things* (1 Corinthians 2:14–15).

There were two trees in the Garden of Eden.

Eating from the Tree of Life would have led to greater spiritual life. The day Adam and Eve ate of the Tree of the Knowledge of Good and Evil, they died *spiritually*. At that point, they were alive *soulically* and *physically* (they had *bios* life and *psuche* life). They had no *spiritual* life. Eating from the Tree of the Knowledge of Good and Evil caused Adam and Eve to become soul-centered or issue-centered. Significantly, psychologists use the expression *ego strength* to define the power of a person to change. The natural man believes in self-sufficiency, e.g., *I can change myself*. While this may seem perfectly natural, it is also perfectly inadequate. A Biblical Counselor leads the counselee back to the *Tree of Life!* Even as God encouraged them to eat liberally from the Tree of Life (representative of Jesus), so years later Jesus would say *unless you eat my flesh and drink my blood, you will have no life* (John 6:53). Obviously, the people Jesus addressed had *natural* life, but they had no *spiritual* life.

BIBLICAL COUNSELING ACKNOWLEDGES THAT *Sin* IS THE REASON FOR OUR ISSUES

The word for "sin" most commonly used in the New Testament means to "miss the mark." Sin is any departure from the commandments, doctrine, or exhortations from the Bible. Peter says sin is anything by which man is enslaved (2 Peter 2:19). In his natural sinful state man is not capable of any spiritual good—Isaiah says *[man's] righteousness is as filthy rags* (Isaiah 64:6); and Paul states "nothing good dwells in me, that is my flesh" (Romans 7:18). So, the Biblical counselor understands that just as no one is saved except by grace (Ephesians 2:10) so no one can be changed or transformed except by a work of God's grace. This basic tenet of Biblical counseling opposes the assumption of psychology that human problems can be purely psychological in nature, unrelated to spiritual things. Even more significantly, secular psychology is premised on the inherent goodness of man and his ability to change.

BIBLICAL COUNSELING ACKNOWLEDGES THAT MAN IS DESIGNED TO BE *SPIRITUAL*

We must pause for a moment here to note the difference between our soul and spirit. Unfortunately, this is a point of dispute among theologians. As a Biblical counselor—and having been trained in psychology as well—I believe the teaching of tri-part man and consequent distinguishing of soul and spirit is vital to understanding God's design for humanity. Any view of *self* that does not recognize the spirit as a separate part (as well as the best and most uplifting part) of man is incomplete and inadequate. But more importantly, it causes "identity confusion."

Our human spirit is made alive—quickened—by the indwelling of Jesus Christ (Ephesians 2). This is called the new birth (John 3:6–7). Thus made alive by the life of Jesus Christ, the human spirit becomes the means through which the Holy Spirit seeks to influence and repossess the soul—one's mind, emotions, and will. For this reason, it becomes very difficult in certain Scriptures to distinguish between the human spirit and the Holy Spirit. The translators frequently have a problem to determine whether to spell the word *spirit* with a capital letter 'S' or a small letter 's.' Regardless, our renewed spirit is fully subject to the control of the Holy Spirit, so that Spirit and spirit are in union. One cannot be born again without the spirit/Spirit relationship (Romans 8:16: *The Spirit Himself bears witness with our spirit that we are the children of God*).

Having been born again, believers have been *organically* changed by the new birth, referred to as the *new creation* (2 Corinthians 5:17). To counsel a spiritual person as though he were a natural person is nonsense. The pursuit of truth and wholeness is a quest of one's spiritual personhood, ultimately an understanding of his new nature: he is IN Christ.

BIBLICAL COUNSELING IS CROSS-CENTERED

*The word of the cross is foolishness to those who are perishing, but to those who are being saved it is the **power of God** . . . may it never be that I should boast, except in the cross of our Lord Jesus Christ, through which the world has been crucified to me, and I to the world . . . for I have been crucified with Christ and it is no longer I who live, but Christ lives in me.*

(1 Corinthians 1:18; Galatians 6:14; 2:20)

The underpinning of *effective* and *strategic* Biblical counseling is the finished work of Jesus Christ on the cross. The believer's union with Christ—through His death and resurrection (Romans 6:1–14)—results in the power to live a satisfying and victorious life in a fallen world. The cross is the answer to sin: inadequate human effort, weakness, and suffering. The cross is the source of the believer's victory. We will explore this theme in detail in chapter 6.

The Cross is a Proclamation

The Biblical counselor makes a proclamation to the counselee: Christ's death on the cross means freedom. Through Christ's death, believers are severed from all legal attachment to Adam. And instead, the believer is attached to Christ in an eternal, living, and fruitful union (Rom 6:5–9; 7:4). The cross takes the believer out of Adam and places him in Christ. *Old things are passed away* and can exert no more power in the life of the believer; *all things are now new* (2 Corinthians 5:17). This is not an easy truth for many counselees to receive: their self-image is that of being *in Adam*, rather than *in Christ* (2 Corinthians 5:16).

The Cross is a Process

The Biblical counselor leads the counselee to enter into the process—or application—of the cross—from proclamation that we are *dead to sin* (Romans 6:11) to the process of *dying* to sin (Romans 6:13; 2 Corinthians 4:10–11; Galatians 2:20). Biblical counselors lead the counselee to discover genuine life in Christ through death to the old ways of his "Adamic" life.

> *We are under obligation, not to the flesh, to live according to the flesh—*
> *for if you are living according to the flesh, you must die; but if by the*
> *Spirit you are putting to death the deeds of the body, you will live . . .*
> *and put off the old self which is being corrupted . . . and be renewed in*
> *the spirit of your mind . . . and put on the new self.*
> (Romans 8:12–13; Ephesians 4:22–24)

What is this *old self* the believer is commanded to put off? It is the *Adamic* ways of thinking and acting that the natural man has developed to survive in a fallen world. Some people call them survivor skills, or coping mechanisms. As long as we live as "survivors," we remain under the control of our flesh. What is flesh? (We will explore this theme in chapter 7.) The flesh can be defined as those self-efforts wherein one attempts to live out of his own resources to meet his needs. While man's *old self* was legally put to death with Christ's death and burial (Romans 6:4, 6), the *flesh* remains as residual. As the cross is applied to the counselee's self-life/flesh, as the old self is *put off* by the process of mind renewal, and as the new self is *put on*, the counselee will experience *resurrection life*: a life of power, confidence, joy, and peace. He no longer sees himself as a *survivor*, but an *overcomer*. The Biblical counselor helps to identify the counselee's fleshly structure with its passions and desires (Galatians 5:24).

Without the power of the cross, counselors are ineffective. Why is it that so many counselors have come to rely on natural methods? The only reasonable explanation is that Christians have become so accustomed to operating out of their natural and mental capacities they do not know the difference.

Biblical Counseling is the Authority of the Believer

Our sinful nature (*flesh*) alone cannot explain the depths of sinfulness in the world. The Bible clearly presents a **warfare worldview**—the world is engaged in a cosmic war between a myriad of agents, both human and angelic, that have aligned themselves with either God or Satan. Jesus unequivocally opposed evils such as disease, demons, and even natural disaster (Jesus rebuked the storm) as originating in the will of Satan, fallen angels, and sinful people.

While the Bible clearly espouses a battle between good and evil, it declares God's sovereignty. Believers are assured of God's victory, already won in the sinless sacrifice and resurrection of Christ (Col. 2:13–14). But since the demise of evil has not yet been fully realized, Christians are called to wage spiritual warfare (Eph. 6:10–17) against evil through intercessory prayer.

The Biblical counselor possesses divinely powerful weapons for the work of destroying the "strongholds" of the flesh. The weapons are the Word and prayer. The believer's *priesthood* (1 Peter 2:9) is fundamental to the Biblical counseling ministry. Like the Old Testament *priests*, Biblical counselors intercede for their counselees. And in so doing, they invest in their lives. They become a vessel of spiritual authority—speaking truth to set the captive free (Luke 4:18; Matthew 16:18–19).

Satan's warfare strategy is to cause a believer to become discouraged and lose hope (Galatians 6:9). Counselees often begin counseling at a low point of faith. The enemy has numbed them into a coping kind of Christianity; they have given up the hope of seeing God's resurrection power in their lives. Only through aggressive warfare prayer can these demonic influences be put to flight. That is a primary strength and advantage of the Biblical counselor.

A FINAL WORD ABOUT BIBLICAL COUNSELING VERSUS PSYCHOLOGY

Since I began this chapter by referring to the distinctions between psychological counseling and Biblical counseling, allow me a few concluding statements.

Psychology does provide some insight about human behavior. In Biblical language, we could say psychological studies help us understand the *old self*. Yes, psychology helps us understand the issues. But psychology is issue-centered, and therefore, incomplete. Compared to Biblical counseling, I therefore conclude that psychotherapeutic models are incomplete in three ways.

1. They do not convey *full* truth (God is excluded)
2. They are inadequate to produce *real* change (eternal value)
3. They cannot produce the *true quality* of life (eternal life)

In summary, Biblical Counseling is about relationship with Jesus; the goal of Biblical counseling is Christ-likeness.

QUESTIONS:

What is the difference between a psychological framework and a Biblical framework?

Why is it important to "use" the Word of God in counseling?

What is the role of the Holy Spirit in Biblical counseling?

Why is it important to emphasize the distinction between the soul and the human spirit?

What does this statement mean: Biblical counseling is not "natural"?.

What does Biblical counseling focus on instead of issues?

What is the significance of a warfare "worldview?"

CHAPTER TWO

What is a Biblical Counselor?

Brethren, even if a man is caught in a trespass, you, who are spiritual, restore such a one, in a spirit of gentleness, each one looking to yourself, lest you too be tempted . . . bear one another's burdens and thus fulfill the law of Christ . . . each one shall carry his own load.

(Galatians 6:1–2, 5)

G od's ultimate purpose is to reconcile men to Himself through redemption. Redemption is followed by restoration, the ministry given to the New Testament believers. No other passage in the Pauline epistles better defines the role, the process, and the goal of the Biblical counselor, herein described as **restoration** and **burden bearing**. With regard to the former, there are six characteristics that delineate the ministry of restoration in Galatians 6:1. When a counselor is aligned with these principles, he will be assured of bearing lasting fruit in his counselee's life.

1. Biblical Counselors are committed to the Weak and Faint-hearted

Mature believers are called to help those *caught in a trespass*. In the Greek language, the word evokes an image of an animal caught in a snare, hurting and fearful, needing to be rescued. The Greek word suggests surprise. Restoration is the divinely designed response of the Body of Christ to those who have been **surprised** by temptation and fallen into sin. There are other Scriptures that call upon mature members to rebuke those who are willfully disobedient, even to disassociate from them. In 1 Thessalonians 5:14, Paul tells the mature Christians to *rebuke the unruly, encourage the fainthearted, help the weak, and be patient with all.* The *faint-hearted* and *weak* are those who are *caught*, and in need of restoration. The person who is *caught in a trespass* is the one who says, *I don't know why I am doing what I am doing, but I really do want to stop doing it. I want to change, but don't know how. Please help me.* He is stuck in his spiritual growth. He is looking for insight, encouragement, hope and motivation. A primary role of the Biblical counselor is to help the counselee understand **why** he continues to get caught.

Trespass means to "miss the mark." The doctrine of sin or viewing all men as *sinners* is fundamental to Biblical counseling. Through Adam and Eve, all mankind inherited a sin nature (Romans 3:23; 8:7). Thus, they suffer; they have conflicts and problems. Their conflicts and problems are rooted in sin. This understanding of pathology (a psychological term for "what's wrong") is foundational. Why? It is essential to our success in helping hurting people that we operate in the knowledge of universal sin. A generation of Christians has emerged who want to re-label their sinfulness with words like *dysfunction, disorders, mental illnesses, neuroses* and *psychoses*. The American Psychiatric Association's *Diagnostic and Statistical Manual of Mental Disorders* has several hundred listings of abnormal human behaviors. Within the Body of Christ, there is a prescribed method for dealing with dysfunction!

Confess your sins to one another, and pray for one another so that you may be healed .

(James 5:16)

2. Biblical Counselors are Spiritually Mature

The call of Biblical counseling is to *you who are spiritual*. In 1 Corinthians 2:15, Paul makes a profound statement: *the spiritual man has the mind of Christ*. When a person is born again his spirit is brought to life by the indwelling Holy Spirit. All the power and resources of the Holy Spirit are available to him to function as God intended. These resources are known as the *gifts of the Spirit* and the result is the *fruit of the Spirit*. The Biblical counselor does not rely upon his own understanding (Proverbs 3:5) but upon the Spirit's discernment and wisdom.

Many times people ask the question: is there a *spiritual gift* of counseling? There is no particular gifting that is essential for counseling. If a person's primary spiritual gift is *teaching* he will be a teaching-type of counselor. If his gift is *mercy* he may be a good listener and show great empathy. If his gift is *exhortation* he may inspire and challenge his counselee to greater heights. A person's primary gift and collections of gifts determine what kind of counselor he will be. The gifts that are most common to those who desire to be counselors are: teaching, pastoring, healing, faith, discernment and mercy. But regardless of the gifting, the Biblical counselor recognizes the Spirit's anointing for the purpose of counseling. And most importantly, he has reached a point of maturity in exercising those gifts.

3. Biblical Counselors Make Spiritual Adjustments

The fundamental meaning of the word **restoration** is "to adjust, to fit, to finish, or to put a thing in its appropriate position." (Doesn't that sound like something a chiropractor does?)

In the Gospels the word *restore* is used to mean "the mending of broken and torn nets." In this verse, it is used to mean "to adjust or repair a thing to its original and proper use." The same word is translated *complete* in Paul's first letter to the believers at Thessalonica. He says *night and day we kept praying most earnestly that we may see your face, and may* **complete** *what is lacking in your faith* (3:10). Paul feared that wherever their knowledge of God was incomplete, they were vulnerable to the enemy's attacks.

The natural man spends his lifetime building up elaborate psychological defenses to convince himself he is a not inadequate. But the natural man is incomplete. All those who are part of God's *new creation* are called to help one another enter into the *wholeness* and *completeness* of being *in Christ*. In Colossians 2:10, Paul declares that all the fullness of God dwells in believers: *by His fullness we have been made complete*. A primary goal of the Biblical counselor is to help his counselee stop paying attention to his deficits, and pay attention to the fullness within him. The Biblical counselor must be able to discern where the counselee is still incomplete in his understanding. Where a believer is incomplete and lacking in faith he will be vulnerable to temptation.

4. Biblical Counselors are Gentle

As previously stated, Biblical counselors understand that their counselees are *caught in a trap*. The emotional pain of this is almost unbearable. Counselees feel like failures. With a spirit of gentleness, counselors are the instruments of God's love and comfort (2 Corinthians 1:4). Paul reminds the believers they should always deal tenderly with those overcome by sin. They are to cultivate the compassion of the Lord as they minister to the weak and faint-hearted, never as one who triumphs in a brother's fall, but rather as one who mourns with him.

A bruised reed He will not break (Isaiah 42:3; Matthew 12:20) takes on special meaning when applied to the role of the Biblical counselor. A bruised reed is one that is not of any use, only to be tossed out.

But the prophet Isaiah declares that the Messiah will take special interest in them. There are many passages in the Old Testament where Jesus is likened to a shepherd who will come and rescue the sheep that have been neglected and abused by their "false shepherds" (Jeremiah 3:15; 23:1–4). These false shepherds do not *strengthen the sick, heal the diseased, bind up the broken, bring back the scattered, or seek the lost.* But of Jesus, Isaiah says *Like a shepherd He will tend His flock. In His arms He will gather the lambs, and carry them in His bosom; He will gently lead the nursing ewes* (Isaiah 40:11). These "bruised reeds" are people in a fragile condition because the enemy has beaten them up. The *bruised reed* passage speaks of the way the Lord will lead His people out of enemy captivity. Similarly, Paul expressed this same concept to the New Testament shepherds:

> *And the Lord's bond servant must not be quarrelsome, but be kind to all, able to teach, patient when wronged, with gentleness correcting those who are in opposition, if perhaps God may grant them repentance leading to the knowledge of the truth, and they may come to their senses and escape from the snare of the devil, having been held captive by him to do his will .*
>
> (2 Timothy 2:24–26)

5. Biblical Counselors Must Practice Self-Examination

The Biblical counselor is committed to his own spiritual progress. This calls for disciplined living. As a spiritual leader, he studies, prays, and seeks correction. He searches the Scripture for insights from the Lord—for himself and for his counselees. He is an example to other believers (1 Timothy 4:12). He is committed to live by the truth he teaches; Paul tells Timothy to *pay attention* to his own teaching to assure *salvation both for himself and for those who would hear [it]* (1 Timothy 4:16). The Biblical counselor "looks to himself." The Greek word for *look* is *skopeo.* Related to our English word *scope,* the meaning is to *spy out.* The Biblical counselor examines his motives, feelings, and attitudes. As the Biblical counselor commits himself to a daily time of Bible reading and meditation, reflection and prayer, the Holy Spirit Himself will expose the things in his heart that might prevent him from hearing the Lord, or expose the pockets of pride that will keep God's work from being accomplished. Like David, he says *examine me and see if there is some hurtful way in me* (Psalm 139:23–24). The writer of Hebrews explains what will happen when God's Word is allowed to search one's heart. It reveals one's thoughts and intentions. While heart work may be hard work, we can be assured that it is His work!

> *The word of God is living and active, and sharper than a two-edged sword, and piercing as far as the division of soul and spirit, of both joints and marrow, and able to judge the thoughts and intentions of the heart.*
>
> (Hebrews 4:12)

6. Biblical Counselors are Humble

Spiritually mature believers who restore others are cautioned to be careful lest they be overtaken in a fault too. Thus, it behooves any one who desires to be a counselor to know his own weaknesses, and to be cautious and guarded against his own temptations: *Keep watching and praying lest you enter into temptation* (Matthew 26:41). As the Biblical counselor is exposed to the hidden faults in others, his own sinful attitudes may be stirred up. There is a tremendously subtle temptation toward spiritual pride. Therefore he must be sensitive to the Spirit's correction. *God is opposed to the proud, but gives grace to the humble* (James 4:6). *To this one I will look, to him who is humble and contrite of spirit, and who trembles at My word* (Isaiah 66:2). To be effective, then, the Biblical counselor must cultivate a humble and teachable spirit to watch over his own heart: *Take the log out of your own eye first before you try to take a speck out of someone else's* (Matthew 7:5).

The Goal of the Biblical Counselor: Equip the Counselee to Carry His Own Load

Bear one another's burdens, and thus fulfill the law of Christ . . . and each one shall carry his own load.

(Galatians 6:2, 5)

In their *corporate-ness*, believers feel each others' pain. And if one member suffers, all the members suffer too (1 Corinthians 12:26). The law of Christ requires each member of the Body to help carry the burden of a suffering brother or sister.

But, this duty in no way diminishes the personal responsibility of each Christian to carry his own load. In Galatians 6:2 and 5, Paul insightfully addresses both the issues of mutual responsibility and progressive independence for believers. Paul's words exhort Biblical counselors to discern the difference between burdens and loads.

The words used for *burden* and *load* in verses 2 and 5, respectively, are different words in the Greek, though they are often used interchangeably in English. The word for *burden* in verse 2 is the Greek word *baros*; the Greek word in verse 5 is the word *phortios*. And though the words are often used interchangeably, a careful word study distinguishes their difference.

Burden

The word *baros* suggests excessive heaviness, too much for one to carry. The responsibility and privilege of every believer—as part of his calling to the *royal priesthood*—is burden bearing. He must help to carry that which would overcome a brother if he had to carry it alone. Paul's attitude is expressed in his letter to the Colossians: *I labor, struggling . . . for I want you to know how great a struggle I have on your behalf. Now I rejoice in my sufferings for your sake, and in my flesh I do my share on behalf of His body* (Colossians 1:24, 2:1).

In the sphere of the Body of Christ, there exists the entire range of believers in various stages of development. The stronger are to protect and nurture the weaker. Is this not what Jesus must have intended when He said, *to the extent that you did it to one of these brothers of Mine, even the least of them, you did it to Me* (Matthew 25:40)? Jesus accused the Pharisees of laying heavy burdens (*baros*) on the Jews (Luke 11:46).

Load

Paul uses the word *phortios* when he says each one is to carry his own *load*. Whereas *baros* is a load one is not expected to carry, relative to his maturity level or his spiritual capacity, a *phortios* is a load he is capable of carrying. At any given developmental stage each person will have trials too difficult to bear alone. But on the other hand, it would be irresponsible of a believer not to carry that which he is capable of. Jesus uses the word *phortios* when He says, *my yoke is easy and my burden* (phortios) *is light* (Matthew 11:29–30).

THE DIFFERENCE BETWEEN A BURDEN AND A LOAD

Since it is a commandment that each one carry his load, it is essential that Biblical counselors discern the difference between burdens and loads. In the larger context of this passage, it is apparent that Paul is addressing those who are *spiritual: You who are spiritual restore such a one*. And *such a one* refers to those who are *caught in a trespass*. So, Paul is addressing the more mature members to help those who are less mature, those more prone to fall into sin. There are two categories: those who fall, or stumble, and those who restore them. Relative to the member's age (spiritual maturity level) there will be a dependency need or an expectation of independence. One will be a *burden bearer* while another will need his burden carried. And the expectation is that each one will grow in capacity to carry his load.

An effective Biblical counselor discerns the maturity level of his counselee and will take precaution not to create a dependent relationship. A word of caution is necessary to those involved in the ministry of *burden bearing*. It is for people who are natural people helpers. They love to *nurture* those who love to be *nurtured*! They are "rescuers." It is meeting the need of the burden bearer: it makes him feel good about himself. Pastors and counselors must be very careful of these natural tendencies: they do not serve the counselee's best interest. It is *not* the role of the Biblical counselor to take care of a weaker brother. The effective Biblical counselor leads the dependent counselee out of dependence on others to dependence on the Lord. This is the goal of restoration: *each one shall carry his own load.*

QUESTIONS

What are the six components of the ministry of "restoration" found in Galatians 6:1?

Why is self-evaluation important for the Biblical counselor?

What is the difference between a load and a burden?

How will you keep your counselee from becoming dependent on you?

CHAPTER THREE

Who am I?

Scenario:

Early in my counseling career, a 20-year old college student named Gerald was referred to me. Gerald was struggling with depression and suicidal thoughts. As he entered my office, I was struck by his appearance: he was definitely bi-racial: African American and Caucasian, he had light brown skin with freckles and reddish hair. Growing up in Harlem, Gerald was taunted and teased for his physical differences. He felt rejected by the other boys. Growing up in a household of women, and having no father figure to model masculinity, he developed a gender confusion that is not unusual for someone with his background—he had sexualized his longing for a strong man in his life. Gerald's anxiety and depression stemmed from his feelings of guilt and inadequacy as a man. In short, Gerald was conflicted about his identity.

From the first appointment, the counselor begins to evaluate the counselee's self-image and self-esteem. The first—and arguably the most important—objective in Biblical counseling is to help the counselee make a connection between his negative feelings, problem behaviors and self-image. Every person's self-image is a reflection of his background. A believer's identity is rightfully an expression of his being a child in God's family. However, most counselees are conflicted, seeing themselves through their histories. The counselee is still subjectively identifying himself as the sum total of his life experiences. To put it in Paul's words (Romans 12:2), he has been **conformed** to (formed by) his "world," i.e., his life experiences. A primary task of the Biblical counselor is to assist the counselee to make the transformation from this *old* way of seeing himself to a *new* way (2 Corinthians 5:16–17).

Therefore, in order to addresses the fundamental issue of one's identity, the Biblical counselor will need to know what the Bible says about *self-image*. The Bible provides the answers needed to develop a *framework* that defines what it is to be a *whole* person. Only the Bible can define what it means to be fully human. And conversely, the Bible defines what it means to be less than fully human, incomplete, or in the modern-day vernacular, "dysfunctional."

When God created the world, he designed *man* to be the centerpiece. To understand God's design, we must examine the first few chapters of Genesis to learn what took place *in the beginning*. This is called the *law of first mention*. In these first chapters of the Bible, we gain understanding of these operational relationships between God and man and between men and women as originally intended. Accordingly, God's first recorded statement about the creation of the first man will be the foundation upon which we build our theological framework for understanding "man" (to be used generically from hereon, speaking of men and women).

WHAT IS OUR SELF-IMAGE?

Let Us make man in Our image.

(Genesis 1:26)

Created in the image of God and placed in the Garden of Eden, Adam and Eve were not conflicted about their self-image. They were not troubled with low-self esteem. They did not have an inferiority complex. They had no parents to blame for anything! They did not think it presumptuous to say: "I bear the image of God." And their actions, feelings, and thoughts reflected this likeness.

But as soon as they departed from the path God had chosen for them, Adam and Eve were separated from God; this *image of God* was spoiled; and their identity was radically altered. Adam's humanity—his identity—was intended to be inseparable from his divinity. The link was broken. He became estranged from his innermost self. I can just imagine "Who am I" must have been the first words out of Adam's mouth. And the second words, as he looked at Eve, were probably "And who are you?" Consequently, all men are born in identity crisis because man cannot know himself apart from God. Man cannot possibly experience the good self-esteem that God intended, apart from a relationship with God. And in man's quest for understanding his identity apart from God, all manner of dysfunction is evident. One need look no further than the first half of the book of Genesis to find anger, murder, revenge, bigamy, violence, drunkenness, sensuality, pride, over-achievement, lying, rape, and war.

Our **natural** identity is acquired from our parents or other formative influences (Exodus 34:7; Proverbs 1:8; John 8:44). These *Adamic* family systems have a certain authority over us and have been the breeding ground for the rational, emotional, and behavioral patterns that form our concept of personal identity. This is why Paul says in Romans 12:2 **not** to be *conformed to this world* [these family influences] because they do not define who we are.

Perhaps it will be helpful to compare the divergent schools of psychology to understand how they deal with the concept of identity. For the purpose of this comparison, psychotherapies will be viewed through three broad categories, or schools of thought.

Cognitive Restructuring or Cognitive-Behaviorism

This general approach of psychology concentrates on cognition and defines problem behavior as "mental problems," i.e., disordered thinking by which persons consistently distort reality in a self-defeating manner. These thought distortions result in unpleasant emotions and unwanted behaviors. The goal of such therapy is to change one's belief system. With respect to *identity*, they might say, *You are what you think*.

Behaviorism

The theoretical framework of psychotherapies that focuses on behavior is grouped under the heading of "behavioral psychology." These counselors focus on volition, or the "will," as the key to identity. They might say, *You are what you do*. Behaviorists employ a number of specific techniques—the most common of which is known as "behavior modification."

Primal or Rational Emotive Therapies

Still other psychologists focus on techniques that release the emotions, providing cathartic experiences that purge one of negative feelings. This order of psychology is called Primal Therapy. A combination of cognitive restructuring and emotionally oriented therapy is called Rational Emotive which recognizes the effect of negative thinking on the emotions. In terms of identity, they might say, *You are what you feel*.

Mind, Emotion, and Will as a Working Definition

Very simply, these three schools of psychotherapy represent three different theoretical frameworks that show how psychology views identity. Before you accuse me of oversimplification, let me note that all theoretical frameworks incorporate some combination of the mental, volitional, and emotional aspects of man. Although the Bible also identifies that mind, emotions, and will have something to do with our identity, any model that only includes these three components is incomplete.

WHAT IS GOD'S IMAGE?

To reiterate our central premise, man was created in God's image. Let's examine this further. Image speaks of that which can be seen. The American Dictionary of the English Language, by Noah Webster, defines *image* as: *the representation of a person or thing, formed of material substance.* God does not have material substance, as we know it. He is called the "invisible" One (Colossians 1:15). God's image is not of the material world: He is Spirit (John 4:24). All who occupy the "unseen" realm are spirits. In the gospel of John, Jesus explains that those who desire to have relationship with God must do so in the spiritual realm, not the material realm, because God is Spirit.

While God possesses the capacities of the human soul—He thinks, feels, and decides—God's image cannot be merely psychological. Why? The Apostle Paul says God does not relate to man through the "psyche," his natural thoughts and affections; He relates to man through his spirit (1 Corinthians 2:11). That God is Spirit, then, is the essence of who God is. This is the all-governing principle: God is Spirit. And He is the father of spirits (Hebrews 12:9).

GOD'S ORDER: SPIRIT, SOUL, BODY

The Lord God formed man from the dust of the ground and breathed into his nostrils the breath of life and he became a living being."
(Genesis 2:7)

In this *first mention* verse are the three components of man's being. These three phases of his creation illustrate God's order. First, man has a body made out of the physical substance we call "earth." Next, God breathed into his nostrils the "breath of life." Throughout Scripture breath and/or air is indicative of *spirit*. Then, man became a "living being." The word for *living being* in the Greek translation would be *psuche*, i.e., the soul. The union of earthly substance (body) and divine breath (spirit) produced life (soul). The body became animate; the soul became conscious. Body and soul derive life from divine Spirit.

God is Spirit and those who worship Him must do so in spirit . . . (John 4:24). The Holy Spirit reveals that those who communicate and fellowship with God must be constitutionally spiritual since God is Spirit. God accomplished this by giving man a human spirit. Having been created spirit, soul, and body, it is the human spirit that enables man to have relationship with the Creator. God gave man a soul, his personality, allowing him to be a unique individual with senses or abilities for thinking, feeling and acting. He designed housing, the body, that was intended to respond to those faculties through the five senses. This was the whole person as God created him: the highest order of his identity, then, was Adam's spirit-to-Spirit relationship with God. And to that Spirit-to-spirit relationship, the soul was subordinated and the body functioned accordingly. This is divine order (see diagram 1).

GOD DEFINES WHOLENESS

Now may the God of peace Himself sanctify you entirely; and may your spirit and soul and body be preserved complete without blame at the coming of our Lord Jesus Christ.

(1 Thessalonians 5:23)

Paul's prayer in this verse captures the essence of wholeness through a number of carefully chosen words. First, notice the order of one's personhood as described here: spirit, soul, and body. The expression most commonly used is "body, soul and spirit." The natural person relates to others physically, socially, intellectually, emotionally and volitionally (all elements of soul/body personhood). But the natural man sees spiritual relationship as optional. However, Paul's description of man is deliberate: man is first a spiritual being, then a psychological/physical being. And man is not a whole being until he is born again, born of the Spirit: he is a "spirit-soul-body" person.

In this verse the word used to indicate *wholeness* is the word *sanctify*, meaning *to set something apart for its intended purpose*. Therefore, the significance of the word *sanctify* is that God intends that "spirit-centered, spirit-empowered" people are those who function the way God intended. The word "entirely," added to the end of the phrase, means *whole* or *complete*. Literally, it means all the parts are there. This simply amplifies the concept that man is not complete unless there is integration of his spirit, soul, and body. And finally, the phrase *preserved complete* adds another dimension to the idea of wholeness. The expression is that God is not finished with a man until he is a spirit-controlled being who reflects God's life in the physical world, through his thoughts, choices, and feelings.

GOD DEFINES THE SOURCE OF LIFE

For the word of God is living and active and sharper than a two-edged sword, and piercing as far as the division of soul and spirit, of both joints and marrow and able to judge the thoughts and intentions of the heart.

(Hebrews 4:12)

In this verse, the writer of Hebrews speaks of the dynamic operation of the Word of God. The Word penetrates into the soul and spirit, dividing the two, so that man is able to distinguish between the *soulical* and the *spiritual*, distinguishing thoughts deriving from his own mind versus those that emanate from the Spirit of God. Significantly, the writer compares the soul to joints and the spirit to marrow. Marrow is where blood is produced; it is literally the source of life. The joints are the outward, visible activity of a healthy person. Thus, the writer is saying that life begins in the spirit and is manifested in the soul or personality. The Holy Spirit whose dwelling place is the human spirit is the source of life (John 7:38).

Natural versus Spiritual

*The **natural** man does not accept the things of the Spirit of God for they are foolishness to him and he cannot understand them because they are spiritually appraised. But He who is **spiritual** appraises all things.*

(1 Corinthians 2:14–15)

The Greek language enlightens one's understanding of these two types of persons: the natural and the spiritual. The Greek word for *natural man* is *psuchikos*. The root of **psuchikos** is *psyche* from which we get our word psychology. Natural man is **psuchikos**. The suffix *ikos* means "under the control of" or "belonging to." Therefore, the natural man is under the control of his psuche, his soul. Psychology, quite literally then, is the study of man's psyche or man's soul.

The Greek word for *spiritual man* is **pneumatikos** (*pneuma*: spirit). The spiritual man is under control of the spirit. So Paul refers to these believers who have been born again as *spiritual*. God's original creation was a man under the control of God's Spirit.

A Final Word about Identity

Understanding one's correct identity is the beginning of change. Every counselee must put off the old way of thinking of himself and put on the new way God sees him. Until that happens, any changes will be superficial, not really dealing with the underlying concern. Counselees must know this truth: *But as many as received [Christ] to them gave He the authority to become the children of God* (John 1:12). This is the truth: I have been made a child of God. I am part of God's family. And I reflect His image.

I will never forget the first time I understood this truth. I realized for the fist time that my identity had changed from that of "son of Adam" to the "son of God." All of my life I had been clinging on to an *old* way looking at myself. I don't know how many times I had read *If any one is in Christ he is a new creature, old things have passed away; behold! All things have become new* (2 Corinthians 5:17). I had been trying to change without realizing I was already *changed* in Christ. We will explore this theme in greater detail in chapter 6, "Can I Change?"

Back to Gerald

As Gerald began to see that his identity was not to be defined by his race, and that manhood was not defined by his culture, he relaxed into the truth, knowing who God made him to be. Though his feelings of rejection were slow in catching up to the truth, Gerald made progress in counseling once his identity was understood.

WHO AM I?

The Spirit was created as the most central part of our identity by which we commune with God. Our needs are met in relationship with Him.
...the Lord...forms the spirit of man within him.
Zechariah 12:1

Human Spirit

The Soul was created to relate to others with the capacity to think, feel & choose. By God's design, the soul is programmed to belong, to be loved, to matter.
And the LORD God formed man...[and] breathed into his nostrils...and man became a living soul" Genesis 2:7

SOUL

Mind: Thinking God's thoughts

Emotions: Sharing God's Feelings

Will: Doing what God wants

The Body was created to be the vehicle through which the spirit/soul relates to people and the environment.
We have this treasure in earthen vessels. 2 Cor. 4:7

BODY

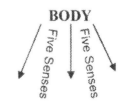

Five Senses   Five Senses

The Physical World

QUESTIONS:

What are God's first recorded words about man?

What does 1 Thessalonians 5:23 tell us about "wholeness?"

What does Hebrews 4:12 tell us about the source of life?

What does Genesis 2:7 tell us about how God designed man?

Do you view yourself as a natural person or a spiritual person?

CHAPTER FOUR

Why did God Make Me?

Scenario

Candy was 20 years old, and caught up in a very bad family situation. Her mother has just left her father who was angry, controlling and abusive. As a result she and her mother and two younger sisters had to move out of a large, beautiful house to a small tract home. She was depressed with her life; everything had changed for the worse.

In the midst of her depressed state, Candy was drawn into a relationship with a neighbor man 12 years her senior. Soon she began to stay most of the time with him. Being a Christian, this became a point of guilt. She justified it because they were planning to get married.

Candy was depressed because she wanted to get married but her boyfriend was reluctant because he was recovering from an injury on the job and was "on disability" and didn't want to get married or set a date until he was able to support her. Meanwhile he was living off his small disability payment in his parents' home. In the course of counseling, I discovered that her boyfriend was a controlling person: they quarreled over the way he wanted things to be done. When Candy came home from work, she would cook dinner for him and take care

,ave him money. In a nutshell, Candy had been drawn
:althy relationship. The question I needed to answer:

/ious chapter, the question "Who am I?" has been answ⟨ ⟩.⟩ 1. Man is the centerpiece of creation. He is God's offspring. He is a spiritual being capable of relationship with God, expressing himself through his spirit, soul and body. This next question is equally important to our understanding of humanity: "What was God's intention in bringing mankind into existence?" Or we might say: "Why is man?" The answer is found quite simply in three fundamental truths.

1) God created a people who would belong to Him, reflecting His glorious image throughout His universe, *bringing many sons to glory* (Hebrews 2:10).
2) God created a people who would be the object of His love (John 3:16).
3) God created a people that would become His partners (fellowship with God) in extending His glory in the world (Ephesians 2:10).

Do I belong? Am I loved? Do I matter?

To understand self-image and self-esteem of our counselees it is imperative we consider these questions: As he grew up, *did he feel like he belonged? That he was loved? That he mattered? And what did he do to compensate for those deficits in his life?* These questions reveal the counselee's self-image and self-esteem, deriving from the development of his psyche, or soul. Yes, people were designed to be *spiritual* people. But while *spirit* may be the source of our life, one's identity is worked out through the psyche (thinking, feeling, and choosing). How a counselee expresses himself mentally, emotionally and behaviorally corresponds directly to how the counselee *sees* or *esteems* himself. As will be demonstrated in later chapters, this concept is vital to the Biblical counselor's method of diagnosis.

WHAT IS DYSFUNCTION?

The term "dysfunctional" has become quite commonly used in this generation. Although this term is used casually in popular culture, health care professionals define a dysfunctional person as one whose relationships are not conducive to good mental and physical health. Sexual or physical abuse, alcohol and drug addictions, behavior problems, eating disorders, and extreme aggression or passivity are some conditions commonly associated with dysfunctional persons. Note: dysfunctional persons are generally part of dysfunctional family systems.

There is no strict definition of a "dysfunctional family." The term tends to be a catch-all for many different relational disorders that take place within the family system and its subsystems (parents, children). Family therapists have many different approaches to treatment—psychodynamic, behavioral, cognitive, or a combination of these therapies.

WHAT IS FUNCTION?

Significantly, no one seems to have a clear view of what "function" is and how to define function versus dysfunction. This is where the Biblical counselor comes to a greater appreciation for the *framework* provided by the Bible.

This chapter will define function, as God intended, and lay the foundation for the Biblical counselor's diagnosis. This chapter answers the question: "Why is man?" The three questions asked above are expressed in the following diagram as a way to define man functionally and relationally.

Diagram 2

Basic Human Need	Un-Fulfilled By the Lack of Parental/Familial	Completely Fulfilled by God's
Belonging Genesis 1:26 "Let us make man in Our image…"	Bonding	Commitment Hebrews 13:5 ("I will never leave you…")
Unconditional Love Genesis 3:8a (fellowship with God in the "cool of the day")	Affection/ Acceptance	Love/Acceptance John 3:16; Romans 5:8 ("God so loved us… while we were yet sinners, Christ died for us")
To Matter or be Effective Genesis 2:15 "put him in the Garden to cultivate and keep it"	Affirmation/ Approval	Plan for Our Lives Ephesians 2:10 ("…we are His workmanship… created for good works…")

A Need to Belong

Let Us . . .

Genesis 1:26

This statement declares that God is a *personal* Being. And because He is a Person—not an abstract concept, not an impersonal influence—He can be known. In this statement, he reveals Himself to man as relational.

The word "Us" indicates that God is plural. He has always existed as God the Father, Son and Holy Spirit. Absolutely integrated and in perfect fellowship and union with Himself, God demonstrates relationship. It was thus that God *injected* a **need to belong** into our psychological DNA. God said, *It is not good for man to be alone.* God said, *Go and multiply throughout the earth.* Deliberately God made us—as a reflection of His image—relational: we need to *belong*.

The **need to belong** is the first building block of our self-image. As expressed in Genesis 1:26 where God said, *Let us make man in Our image*, the "Us" and "image" imply belonging. If a man's son looks like him, people will say, "I think he belongs to you." And maybe when he grows up he will have his father's mannerisms. And people will say, "You are your father's son!" It is really simple: people behave and even look like the people they belong to. And it is for this very reason that family systems are important: they influence offspring and give them their sense of identity. God created man to dwell in relationship. And in telling man to multiply and fill the earth, God is asserting that it is our divine nature to be part of community, to belong. Throughout the Old Testament, God speaks through the prophets, affirming His commitment to *My people*, the people who belong to Him.

A Need to Be Loved

The word "Us" implies not only relationship, but also intimacy. One might ask: how is intimacy different from belonging? Well, it's quite possible to belong to a group, a club, or a church without experiencing any intimacy. God created us **to be loved** and accepted in that place we *belong*. We long for unconditional love and acceptance. It establishes and reinforces our sense of worth. Adam had it before the Fall. Imagine the loss of acceptance that caused him to hide from

God after he came into a new identity apart from God. Adam's self-worth was no longer derived from God's image in him.

Throughout Scriptures, God's love is proclaimed. He is the great *agape*. The Greek word *agape* is not romantic love. It means *commitment to another's well being*. God is committed to His created beings and their well being. God demonstrates unconditional love and acceptance (Romans 5:8). We were created to be the recipient of His love. And like God, we love, and desire to be loved.

In Genesis 3:8 we read: *they heard the sound of the Lord God walking in the garden in the cool of the day.* It is almost impossible not to presuppose that it was God's habit to come to the garden in the cool of the day, since after all, they were hiding. What other explanation can there be for their action if not that they were expecting Him. Adam and Eve enjoyed fellowship and intimacy with the Lord God before the Fall. He created them to be loved.

Let me speak as a father. I love my children. It is my God-given responsibility and privilege to nurture, affirm and love them as much as I can! When they were young, every night I spent a little "quality" time with each one before putting him and her to bed so they would know that Daddy loved them. That was very important to me because I knew that as I loved them they would be able to feel loved later by others, and more importantly, by God. And, loved properly and unconditionally, they would be able to love others.

The other aspect of unconditional love is acceptance. Acceptance means I'm OK. There is hardly anything worse than the feeling of rejection. Who can escape childhood without the sting of rejection by one's peers? And how much worse when that rejection comes from a parent or some beloved authority figure? The Hebrew word *hesed* means lovingkindness. The word lovingkindness is used over

250 times in the Old Testament. It means loyalty, steadfastness, and faithful love and stresses the idea of a belonging in a love relationship. In the Psalms, the Lord often refers to His commitment to His Godly ones. The term *Godly ones* is derived from *hesed*; and it refers to those who are the object of His lovingkindness. *The Lord has set apart the godly one for Himself* . . . (Ps. 4:3).

A Need to Matter

Let Us **Make** . . .

Genesis 1:26

The word *make* is significant, revealing that God is dynamic, powerful, and competent. He is "in control." God is Creator: by the power of His word, He *spoke* the world into existence (Psalm 33:6–9). God rejoices in His works because they express His glory. In the book of Genesis, God reveals Himself to man by various names that reflect the attributes that define His character. All of these names indicate His intrinsic worth or value, or, in a more theological word, *glory*. The first truth about God is that He highly esteems Himself! To say that God has a good self-image sounds quite silly. The fact is, He knows His worth and value! He is great! He is glorious! All of creation [His works] is an overflow of His greatness and goodness. The Heavens [His works] declare the greatness, the glory of God. Created in God's image, man has a desire to express this excellence through his work too.

In Genesis 2:15, we read: *The Lord God . . . put [man] in the garden to cultivate it and keep it.* Adam's work was an expression of his self-image. Why? It is certainly not because God needed help in taking care of the earth. God wanted to relate to mankind in this partnership: a partnership that expressed *belonging* and *intimacy*. God's "delight" in partnering with His son as they created the world is expressed in Proverbs 8:29–31: *He set for the sea its boundary so that the water would not transgress His command when He marked out the foundations of the earth; Then I [the Son] was beside Him, a master workman; And I was daily His delight* . . . Every mother who allows her little daughter to help set the table or clean the house knows her young daughter cannot possibly perform the task as well as she could herself. It is not the help the mother seeks; it is relationship. The mother knows that in doing the task, the daughter's personality—her sense of belonging, love and acceptance, worth, and competence—is being formed.

People who feel a lack of belonging and love often compensate by exaggerating this third need. These so-called "workaholics," "high-achievers," and "type-A's" seek to meet their needs through perfection and performance. This need has been perverted when it becomes the strongest part of someone's identity. That's not to say it is unimportant. A major component of our identity is the belief that we are effective, capable or competent—we make a difference in our world. God created us to be people of worth, as we express His image. Oh, how man longs to know that he matters. Certainly Paul speaks to this longing when he declares that *[man is] is God's workmanship, created in Christ Jesus for good works, which He prepared beforehand [before the foundation of the world] that [they] should walk in them* (Ephesians 2:10). As God's workmanship, and accomplishing the work he was given to do, man is in an intimate partnership with God that empowers him and gives God pleasure: . . . *for it is God who is at work in you, both to will and to work for His good pleasure* (Philippians 2:13).

GOD SATISFIED ADAM AND EVE'S NEEDS IN THE GARDEN OF "EDEN"

And the Lord God planted a garden toward the east, in Eden; and there He placed the man whom He had fashioned. And out of the ground the Lord God caused to grow every tree that is pleasing to the sight and good for food . . . Delight yourself in the Lord, and He will give you the desires of your heart.

(Genesis 2:8–9; Psalm 37:4)

The Hebrew Word "Eden" means *Delight* or *Pleasure*

After the creation of Adam, the Scriptures tell us God carefully placed him on the earth in a garden called "Eden." We are told that in the Garden was every good thing man needed for life. We should not overlook the importance of this "goodness" as it affects our theological framework.

The word "Eden" is derived from the same root as the word "delight." More than a *place*, Eden was an *environment* where God purposed for His created beings to find full pleasure with Him and one another. In this environment of delight between the Creator and the creature, God's goodness would be known. And in this environment of delight, Adam and Eve were relationally fulfilled. Their sense of competence was complete as they depended upon and partnered with their Maker. Being assured of God's love and acceptance, they knew their worth. If God said they were good, then it must be true!

The word *Eden*, then, suggests God intended for man to live in an environment in which his God-given needs and desires would be satisfied by God. God looked at all that He made and said: "it is very good." In the Hebrew language, the word *good* can mean *pleasant, beautiful, excellent, lovely, delightful, convenient, comfortable, joyful, fruitful, precious, sound, cheerful, kind, correct, righteous, and moral.* This reveals the heart of God: to do *good* for all His creation. Given this, it is difficult to conceive of any "desire" that could not be satisfied in that environment. Adam's desire to be in a relationship that was satisfying and complete was fulfilled in "Eden." Then in relationship with one another (*they were naked and unashamed*), man and woman were able to express God's goodness and personhood. Adam and Eve's desire for purpose was fulfilled as they *partnered* with God in managing the creation. Their desire for belonging and love were fulfilled as they saw in themselves the glory of God.

Back to Cindy

Candy realized that her sense of "belonging" had never been met by her father who was not only emotionally lacking, but was emotionally abusive. He belittled her through criticism and neglect. Over time, Candy realized she was still trying to get a man, in this case her new boyfriend, who was very much like her father, to pay attention to her. She wanted a man to belong to: a man who would take responsibility for her and meet all of her emotional needs. Not long after, she broke up with her boyfriend and moved into an apartment with Christian girlfriends who filled the emotional gap in her life in a healthier way.

QUESTIONS

What do the words "Let Us" in Genesis 1:26 tell us about God's nature and our need?

What does Genesis 2:15 tell us about God's relationship with us and our need?

What does the phrase in Genesis 3:8: "the Lord God walking in the garden in the cool of the day" imply about Adam and Eve's relationship to God and our need?

How does knowing your identity as a spiritual person affect your relationship with others?

CHAPTER FIVE

What is Wrong with Me?

Scenario:

Joyce was referred for counseling due to depression and anxiety. She had been in a relationship with Harry for nearly 6 years. He was not a believer. He had been a drug user in the past. He had proven to be fairly irresponsible with his finances. He had two children from a former relationship. While she knew she could never marry him, Joyce was unable to break off the relationship. Harry made her feel special: he bought her flowers and told her how much he needed her. He complemented her on her good taste and told her he was proud to be seen with her. Joyce did not see the connection between her depression and her inability to remove herself from this "going-nowhere" relationship. In short, Harry was meeting a need in her life, and she was unwilling to break off the relationship because that need was not being met anywhere else.

THE FALL

Man became independent and self-centered

And you shall be like god.

(Genesis 3:8)

The temptation of Adam and Eve was to be "like God," to be independent, autonomous (self-governing) and self-sufficient. Based on his own rational and volitional powers, man would exercise an authority God never intended. By choosing to live by his natural abilities, he would be effectively eliminating the need for God's rule over his life. So, something more terrible than most humans can ever comprehend happened when Adam and Eve chose to be "their own gods." The following quote from C. S. Lewis, *The Problem of Pain*, says it most eloquently.

> *The process [of man's fall] was not comparable to mere deterioration as it may now occur in a human individual: it was a loss of status as a species. That condition was transmitted by heredity to all later generations, for it was not simply what biologists call an acquired variation. It was the emergence of a new kind of man; a new species, never made by God, had sinned its way into existence. It was a radical alteration of his constitution.*

In being his own god, Adam moved from God-centeredness to self-centeredness. This somewhat-veiled truth is expressed in God's statement: *it is not good* (Genesis 2:18). There is great significance in God's statement that something was "not good." It is this: He alone determines what is *good* or *not good*.

Before, the Fall, how do you suppose Adam and Eve decided what was *good*? Obviously their only reference point was God. There was therefore no conflict between Adam and Eve since they each shared God's thoughts and values. God was the reference point to determine what was good. In fact, in their innocence, Adam and Eve may not even have been aware that something could be "not good."

However, after the Fall Adam and Eve became alive to a new reference point, that being changed from God to man. Adam became his own reference point for deciding what was good—if it was good for him, then it should be good for Eve too! Likewise, Eve decided what was good in accordance to her needs and desires. What Satan had promised had become true: each one was truly his own god. And in becoming independent of God, they also became independent of one another. Self-centeredness was born! After this all men were self-dependent, self-loving, self-willing, and self-seeking. And conflict and chaos were the consequence of *self life* (James 4:1).

Separated from God, Man became Needy

In the day, you eat from it [the tree of the knowledge of good and evil] you will surely die.

(Genesis 2:7)

On the day Adam ate of the Tree of the Knowledge of Good and Evil, he did not die—not physically. But he died spiritually. Their act of sin separated them from God, Who was their life. By this definition, death means to be separated from God. But more importantly, Adam and Eve were cut off from the only One who could meet their needs.

Satan deceived Eve by persuading her that she could experience *good things*, (desirable things) apart from God. In effect, Satan convinced Eve that God's provision was insufficient, even implying that God was *withholding* something good from them. Adam, aligning himself with Eve, sinned. Immediately, they became aware of their neediness (Genesis 3:7). This once-satisfying, all-sufficient relationship with their Creator was broken. Adam and Eve's expulsion from Eden—an actual occurrence—is nonetheless symbolic of the loss of relationship with God. Adam and Eve became painfully aware that God alone could meet their innermost needs. Since all mankind thereafter was born into a sinful environment, rather than Eden, it is impossible to comprehend Adam and Eve's loss. From that time on, "Adam's children" would experience pain and encounter resistance as they worked at the task of earning their daily bread. They would experience the heartbreak of broken fellowship and resultant conflict with their fellow human beings as well.

Outside Eden, Adam and Eve experienced the futility (Ephesians 4:17) of man to meet his needs apart from the life-giving Spirit of God (1 Corinthians 15:45). It is especially significant here to see that man's identity changed at this point. For the first time, God refers to His created beings as *dust* and *flesh* (Genesis 3:19; 6:3), indicating that his reference point for defining life had changed from the spiritual to the material. Quite simply, man became *natural*.

Consequently, Adam and Eve did obtain *knowledge* that made them like a god: they could now discern the existence of good and evil. The problem was they could also be tempted by evil; but they were totally powerless to use that knowledge to overcome evil. Without God's rule, they had no *spiritual* authority or power; they only had knowledge. That is the dilemma of the natural man. Because of "free will" and in charge of his own life, he operates in the realm of his own beliefs and thoughts, follows his own emotions, and does what he wants. The natural man does what seems right in his own eyes. He is his own god, functioning by the control of his natural mind and affections.

However, instead of being freed to experience life, as Satan had promised, they entered into a terrible bondage to their natural (psychological) desires and biological impulses. Instead of becoming master over his body, man became a slave to it. Subsequently, the tremendous fear that was born that day was the recognition they had no power, no ability, to meet their needs.

MAN CANNOT MEET HIS NEEDS

God will deliver the needy when he cries for help.

(Psalm 72:12)

In Eden man had been fully satisfied. But after the Fall, not only is man called *flesh*, but also **needy**. The word *needy* is used over 60 times in the Old Testament. The word refers to man's material, social, and spiritual deficit. In the Sermon on the Mount, Jesus acknowledges the neediness of mankind by addressing the fact that God knows all these things *you have need of.* But Jesus concludes that if we seek first the kingdom of God—the nonmaterial realm—all one's material needs will be taken care of. When Satan tempts Jesus to meet his need for hunger, Jesus responds: *Man shall not live by bread alone but by every word that proceeds from the mouth of God* (Matthew 4:4). When the disciples focused on their hunger, Jesus said, *I have meat to eat that you know not of* (John 4:32). Recognizing the neediness of mankind, Jesus invites man into a relationship where his *real* needs could be fulfilled.

However, it is in natural man's quest to meet his needs that self-image is formed. What a person thinks, or how he sees himself results from the search to satisfy his needs and desires. Before we can complete our theological framework for understanding man, we must consider these two questions: 1) what are our needs? and 2) how are these needs related to the development of our self-image and self-esteem?

THE GOD-GIVEN DESIRE TO BELONG BECOMES AN UNMET NEED

Then God said: it is not good for man to be alone.

(Genesis 2:18a)

Man's aloneness is not good. Aloneness is not consistent with the image of God, Who, as we have already noted, is constitutionally relational. Without a female counterpart, Adam could not fulfill God's command to go and multiply throughout the earth. Nor could he reflect God's image without relationship; he needed to belong to someone. Human beings are social beings, reflecting the very image of God as a social being. Belonging is the "us" feeling experienced when we are united with some person or group of people. Who has not had that feeling at some time in his life that he was *on-the-outside-looking-in?*

So God created Adam with a strong motivation to BELONG. And in response to that motivation, marriage, families, and communities would be formed. But belonging was affected by sin. No family since Adam's Fall has been able to meet this need to belong. Biblical counselors must understand that a counselee's sense of belonging is fundamentally established from infancy to early childhood. If a child feels he is included by family and others, he will experience good feelings of belongingness. However, if he feels excluded, he will feel deficit in the area of belonging. When the need to belong goes unfulfilled, man feels needy.

The Scripture says that Adam and Eve were *naked and unashamed* before they sinned. The word "naked" suggests that they had no barriers between them. There was nothing separating them, no need to self-protect, no pretending, and no concealment. But even more important, they were *unashamed.* This word could be translated by the words "not disappointed." When we give our hearts to people with whom we desire intimacy, we will always experience some degree of disappointment. Adam and Eve had no sense of disappointment. Only after they sinned did their differences become problematic. And they distanced themselves from one another (Genesis 3:20).

Unable to cope with this horrible feeling of separation—from God and from each other—their responses are the archetype of how people still respond today. The first thing they did was to **cover up**. They made "clothes" out of leaves from the Garden. When they heard God coming, however, they felt their coverings were inadequate so they **hid** in the bushes. When confronted by God—*who told you, you were naked?*—Adam diverted attention from his self and avoided responsibility through **aggression**, **blaming** God for giving him this wife in the first place.

Later in this account (Genesis 3:20) Adam gives his wife a name. He calls her Eve. We have to wonder why he did not give her a name before they sinned. Is it possible they were so "one" that the concept of **separate** identity was foreign to them? Identity (who am I?) was simply not even an issue. After they sinned, they felt their separateness; belonging became problematic as they recognized they were two separate people. Even as they hid and covered themselves from God, they hid and covered themselves from each other. The modern-day counterpart of this defense is what we refer to as "distancing" or "avoiding." When two people are unable to close the gap, or distance, between them, they will **separate, isolate** and ultimately **exit** the relationship altogether. I have developed the following acronym to help the reader recall these archetypal responses to neediness.

C Covering up
H Hiding
A Aggressing
S Separating
E Exiting

While these responses to Adam's Fall can be seen in everyone of us, it is also important to see how these responses are distinguished specifically when a need to belong, or a need to be loved, or to matter goes unmet. Understanding these is key to understanding the fundamental responses that all people make when there is a deficit in any one of these needs.

When a person's *need to belong* is not met, he or she may experience an exaggerated need for a partner to fulfill all of his/her unmet expectations. Conversely, he or she may withdraw and isolate his or her self for fear of further rejection. (see Diagram 3)

THE GOD-GIVEN DESIRE FOR UNCONDITIONAL LOVE BECOMES AN UNMET NEED

God's love and acceptance of Adam and Eve is unquestionable. A person's self-esteem (his sense of worth) is related to how "acceptable" he feels. People verify their sense of worthiness by others' positive attitudes toward them. When others disapprove, they feel unloved, unacceptable, and unworthy. A major part of Adam's self-esteem was that he was acceptable to God. Adam felt acceptable because he saw God's excellence in his self. God's unconditional love and acceptance of Adam was evidenced, quite simply and profoundly, by God's word, "it was good." Worthiness (or love and acceptance) is related to belonging. People feel good about themselves when others value their association or friendship. Putting it in modern vernacular, they feel "validated."

In Genesis 3:8 we read, *they heard the sound of the Lord God walking in the garden in the cool of the day.* Though this statement occurs after they sinned, it is the "first mention" of this that we must pay attention to. We can presuppose that since they were hiding, they knew God was coming. By deduction, then, we presuppose that it was God's habit to come to the garden in the cool of the day. And considering the nature of God, one can surmise what they did during this time. Adam and Eve enjoyed fellowship and intimacy with the Lord God. He created them because He loved them, and He created them to love Him. John says, *we [are able to] love, because He first loved us* (1 John 4:19). In Spirit to spirit communion, Adam and Eve were able to enjoy unbroken fellowship with God their Father.

After they sinned, God expelled Adam and Eve from the garden. The withdrawal of God's approval left Adam and Eve with a feeling of guilt and shame. And rightfully so, they felt rejected because they knew they had lost their worthiness. It is important for the Biblical counselor to understand the cause of these unworthy feelings.

When a person's need to *be loved and accepted* is not met, he or she may have an exaggerated need for another's affirmation to prove their worth. They are easily engaged in power struggles over incidental events because of an exaggerated need to be "right." (see Diagram 3)

THE GOD-GIVEN DESIRE FOR PURPOSE (TO "MATTER") BECOMES AN UNMET NEED

God is the Creator: He is omnipotent. Though created in God's image, man is not omnipotent. But his sense of competence is fundamental to his identity. Competence is a sense of ability, adequacy and strength to do the work one has to do. Competence is intrinsically related to one's sense of belonging and worthiness: man needs to know that his existence makes a difference—he matters.

In the Eden environment, Adam reflected God's creative power in doing work. Certainly, God did not need Adam to name the animals and care for the garden. But as a reflection of God, he needed to express himself in power, to be competent. Adam was to be a steward, or manager, over the garden: *the Lord God made man and put him in the garden to cultivate it and keep it.* Adam's work was an expression of his relationship to God, an expression of his identity. When Adam and Eve became separated from God, i.e., no longer belonging and no longer acceptable, their working relationship with God was severed too. They were disconnected from their power supply. So many people who have been hurt because their need to belong and need to be loved has not been met become over-achievers—workaholics—in an attempt to recover this need to matter. In such cases, the need to matter becomes exaggerated; it is the strongest part of a person's identity. God created men and women to know their purpose in life and to know they were empowered to do it (Ephesians 2:10). But God never intended that man would be his own independent power source.

When a person's need to matter goes unmet (feeling criticized or undervalued), he may develop an exaggerated need for self-sufficiency and independence and may strive for perfection. Such people may restrict their lives within comfortable boundaries. In so doing, they are able to maintain control over their environment, increasing the chance for success, and minimizing the risk of failure. (see Diagram 3)

SUMMARY

God knows His children are needy—He made them that way. The human personality cannot survive in an empty, meaningless universe. And He is delighted when His children acknowledge their emptiness and seek Him. This paradigm for Biblical counseling is based on this concept that all problems are a result of one or more unmet needs.

Back to Joyce

When Joyce realized that she was expecting Harry to meet her need to belong and to matter, she began to see that she had a choice to meet these needs in other healthier ways. Joyce's father had ignored her as a little girl. Even though she had tried to obtain his love and approval over the years, he had not responded. In relationship with Harry, she told herself she had found someone to meet that need. Even though Harry was not able to fulfill that need completely, Joyce was willing to settle. Someday maybe Harry would marry her. Even as she never gave up on her belief that her father would love her unconditionally and affirm her, she was not willing to let go of Harry either.

Final Note: I have used this model effectively over many years of counseling. Particularly in marriage counseling, it is my observation that women most often feel deficit in the need to belong. And when that goes unfulfilled a woman begins to question whether her husband "values" her and may conclude that she doesn't matter to him. Conversely, men most often express that they do not feel what they do matters because of what they perceive as an overemphasis by their wives on belonging, i.e., relationship. She values relationship (belonging, worth); he values competence (doing).

QUESTIONS

How does God decide what is "good" for mankind?

How does natural man decide what is "good?"

How do you define "good?"

What are the five defensive actions Adam did after he sinned? (CHASE)

Someone who has never felt like they "belong" might have an exaggerated need for . . .

Someone who felt like they never "mattered" might have an exaggerated need for . . .

Diagram 3

STRATEGIES TO MEET UNMET NEEDS

There is a way which seems right to a man, but its end is the way of death. Proverbs 14:12. Why do you spend ...wages for what does not satisfy?" Isaiah 55:2

Basic Needs	When Needs are Unmet: Behaviors & Strategies	Biblical References
To Belong Commitment Connection Cohesion	• An exaggerated need to connect with a partner who will fulfill all of one's expectations for belonging and commitment • An exaggerated need to separate and isolate from others	Isaiah 62:4 Jeremiah 2:13 Jeremiah 17:5 Matthew 19:29 Psalm 68:6
To Be Loved and Accepted Worth Value	• An exaggerated need for affirmation and personal admiration so that others will prove one's worth • An exaggerated need to be right, easily engaging in power struggles.	Isaiah 2:8 Mat. 23:2-7 John 5:44 1 Cor. 3:21 Galatians 5:20
To Matter Purpose Competence Control Effective	• An exaggerated need for self sufficiency & independence; maintaining distance & separation to feel safe • An exaggerated need for perfection to avoid criticism • An exaggerated need to maintain control over one's life and others	Isaiah 29:13 Isaiah 30:16 Prov. 25:27; 28:26; 29:1 1 Cor. 12:21 2 Cor. 6:12 Galatians 6:3 Rev. 3:17

Diagram 4

WHAT IS WRONG WITH ME?

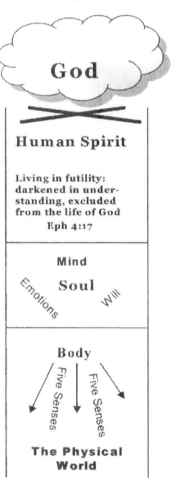

Man is dead in relation to God.
*"You... were dead in
trespasses and sins"*
Ephesians 2:1

Man has a darkened mind and
damaged emotions;
he is self-centered.
*"For the natural man does not
understand the things of God,
for they are spiritually
appraised"*
1 Corinthians 2:14

Man cannot do the "work" that
God created Him to do because
he lives in a sinful environment.
*"By the sweat of your brow
you will eat your food until you
return to the ground"*
Genesis 3:18

CHAPTER SIX

Can I Change?

Scenario:

When Arthur called to make a counseling appointment, he told me that he had just had a conflict with his wife. I could tell that he was embarrassed to talk about their conflict on the phone. When he came in for his first appointment, I learned that Arthur, a 26 year-old man, married for one year, involved in church ministry, was struggling with pornography. When his wife discovered this, she exploded in a rage and then in tears. She felt humiliated. She was angry about his deception. Arthur explained to me that he had been addicted to pornography since he was 12 years old when one day he found his father's Playboy magazines in a closet. He said his father had been addicted to pornography for years and so was his older brother. He could not imagine how he could ever change. Although he had been to church seminars and read books on the subject of sexual addiction, he had experienced little success in overcoming this addiction. He looked at me and said, "I don't think I can ever change. This is just who I am!"

Conflicted people are unhappy. Unhappy people want to change something—about themselves, someone else, or their circumstances. The ultimate question by our counselees is this one: "Can I change?" Then the question is "how?" But before we answer the "how," we must be certain of the "can I . . . ?"

> *If any man is in Christ he is a **new creature**; old things have passed away; behold all things have become new . . . [for] **the old self was crucified with Christ** . . . [so that] we are no longer slaves to sin.*
> (2 Corinthians 5:17; Romans 6:6)

Having been *born again*, every believer is literally part of the *new creation* in Christ! It has been my experience as a pastor and counselor for over 20 years that too many believers do not "know" it. Even if they have been taught this truth, it is not their experience. Despite their best efforts to "walk" the truth, they are focused on their weakness, failure, and defeat. They are too feeling-oriented to receive the truth—their failure to overcome temptation seems to contradict the truth of Paul's words *[you] are a new creature*. Simply put, they do not "feel" like "new creatures." So they disparage God's truth, their identity being tied to their *feelings* rather than God's *facts*.

The doctrinal facts presented by Paul in the sixth chapter of Romans are the bases for the answer to the question "can I change?" How so? The reason we are able to change is that *we are no longer slaves to [controlled by] sin* (Romans 6:6). And why? *[because] the old self was crucified with Christ*. What is this *old self*?

The Old Self is…	Constitutionally Controlled by Sin Part of the Old Creation A Son of Adam, A Child of Disobedience Dead to God, Not yet alive in Christ	Rom. 5:12 Rom. 6:6; Rom. 8:7-17 1 Cor. 15:48-49 Eph. 2:1-2

Since feeling-oriented (fleshly) believers do not "know" this truth, they will ask, "when did this death take place?" The answer: it happened at the cross. Paul explains that when Jesus died, we (born again believers) died with Him, and when Christ was resurrected we were raised up with Him. Though the event happened over 2,000 years ago, at the moment a person accepts Christ as Lord in his life, he is united with Christ.

We are	In His Death on the Cross	
United	In His Burial	Rom. 6:4-6
With	In His Resurrection	Col. 3:1-3
Christ	In His Present Life at the Right Hand of God	

Our union with Christ in His death and resurrection is the doctrinal basis for the answer to the question "can I change?" In the person of Christ, we died to sin's control. Paul restates this throughout his epistles: *the world has been crucified to me, and I to the world* (Galatians 6:14); *I have been crucified with Christ, and it is no longer I who live, but Christ lives in me* (Galatians 2:20); *Consider yourself dead to sin and alive to God* (Romans 6:11); *For you have died and your life is hid with Christ in God* (Colossians 3:3); *If we have died with Christ . . . we shall also live with Him* (Romans 6:8).

The believer's identification with Christ's death and resurrection is possibly the most important truth in the entire Bible. We are no longer slaves to sin . . . yes, we can change because we have been changed. We are *new creatures*, part of the *new creation*. Let us explore this theme.

WHO'S IN CONTROL, ANYWAY?

Let Us make man in Our image, according to Our likeness and let them rule over . . . all the earth . . .

(Genesis 1:26)

The word *rule* means to *exercise control or power over a sphere of influence*. What was Adam and Eve's sphere of influence? They were given control over the earth—but it began in a garden. Adam was given the job of cultivating the Garden of Eden. For most people this may evoke a picture of tranquility and peace. But consider the work involved in a dynamic fruit-bearing environment and a thriving animal population. This was real work! But as they performed their garden activities, Adam and Eve were "in control."

We need to emphasize: **in partnership with God**, Adam was in control. This truth is of great importance to our understanding of "control." But there is another even more significant fact to consider: **Adam did not have to contend with Satan.** He did not yet have a relationship with Satan. And Satan exercised no control over Adam. Relationally speaking, we could say Adam was *alive to God and dead to Satan.*

Adam Loses Control: "Who turned off the power?"

When God placed Adam in the Garden, He said: *in the day you sin you shall surely die.* However, Adam did not die—physically. Adam's death was one of **separation**: sin separated him from God. And in that moment when Adam died relationally to God, he became alive to a new relationship: by sinning, he became alive relationally to Satan. But even more significantly, Adam died to the God-given control over the earth and over himself; sin and Satan now exercised control over him. As the *god of this world*, Satan was in control and *sin ruled* (2 Corinthians 4:4; Romans 5:21). As C. S. Lewis says, *a new kind of man, a new species, never made by God, had sinned its way into existence.*

> *Therefore, just as through one man sin entered into the world, and death through sin, so death spread to all men, because all sinned, sin reigned in death.*
>
> (Romans 5:12, 21)

Therefore, because of sin's control over all who are born from Adam, real change is impossible; the natural man has no power to change (Romans 8:7). He is a slave to sin. It is in control of him. Through sin, Satan's power over man was turned on; God's empowerment of man was turned off.

In Christ, Sin's Control Over Man is Broken

Because of Who *We* Are

The key to understanding our capacity for change is about control. Born into this world through Adam, man is under the control of sin. Without regaining "control" over his self, man cannot change. Paul's question *what shall we say then, are we to continue in sin . . . ?* (Romans 6:1) launches the subject of change.

When Paul says *we* he means

- Those who are *children of God* (John 1:12).
- Those who were part of the new creation (2 Corinthians 5:17)
- Those who are spiritual, not natural (1 Corinthians 2:15)
- Those who have the "mind of Christ" (1 Corinthians 2:16)
- Those who free from sin's control (Romans 6:7, 18)
- Those who are dead to sin and alive to God (Romans 6:11)
- Those who are slaves to righteousness (Romans 6:16)

So Paul says, *How can "we" continue to sin* since "we" are no longer under its control. The answer is not only because of **who we are**, but also because of **where we live**.

Because of *Where We Live*

The answer to Paul's question, *are we to continue in sin . . . ?* is another question, *How shall we who died to sin still live in it?* (Romans 6:2).

Paul presents an illogical and impossible scenario: how could someone be *dead* to sin, and yet still **live** in sin?—Dead and alive at the same time—how could it be possible that *we* who are dead to sin are still living as though *we* are still alive to sin? How can the believer exist in two realities at once? It is impossible!

What does **died to sin** mean? Admittedly, everyone *feels* very much alive to the influence of sin and Satan; therefore, we can deduce that the truth exists apart from *feelings*. Paul explains that believers have died to Satan's rule (the exercise of power and control) over him and have become alive to a new life in Christ. Specifically, the believer has *moved*, as it were from Satan's to God's territory, called the Kingdom of God, *[Christ] has delivered us from the domain of darkness and delivered us into the Kingdom of His beloved Son* (Colossians 1:13).

God's purpose in Christ's death and resurrection was not simply that man should be able to receive forgiveness of his sins, but be able to enter a new **realm** of spiritual experience, *if you have been raised up with Christ, keep seeking the things above . . . [and] set your mind on things above* (Colossians 3:1–2).

Note: The following analogy illustrates this truth. Imagine a person who is a citizen of a country under authoritarian rule, a dictatorship, and moves to the United States. He changes his citizenship from that country to US citizenship. Under a cruel dictatorship, he had been a citizen subject to intimidation and tyranny. He was under the authority of the dictator. But when he left that country and adopted U.S. citizenship, to whom did he become subject? He became subject to the laws of the United States with all of its rights, privileges, and protec-

tions. He would no longer be subject to the laws of that country. He is free! But if he still lived in fear of the dictator, continued to live in the US as though he were still a citizen of that country, afraid and intimidated by the police and authorities, afraid to leave his home, even afraid to go out in public, wouldn't we consider that person to be foolish? Rather than receiving benefit from the laws of the land in which he currently lives, he would be acting like he was still living in and subject to the laws of the authoritarian rule. At the least, we would indeed consider such a person to be neurotic.

How Does the Believer Experientially Break Sin's Control Over Him?

Knowing this, *that our **old self was crucified** with Him that our body of sin might be done away with, that we should no longer be slaves to sin.*

(Romans 6:6)

Diagram 5

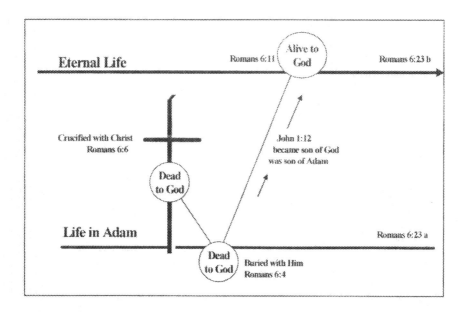

1. By Knowing this Truth: Our Co-crucifixion with Christ

Knowing we can change begins with **knowing** that we are "new" in Christ: our *old self is dead.* This is the truth that underlies the believer's confidence that he can indeed change. Conversely, the root of his inability to change is his **ignorance** of this truth. If he does not know God's truth, he cannot believe it; if he cannot believe it, he cannot experience it. Hosea says *my people are destroyed for lack of knowledge* (4:6). Does your counselee really **know** what God has said about him? Where is a believer's confidence if he does not **believe** that he has been crucified with Christ? Where is his boldness if he does not believe that he died to the control of sin? Where is his faith? It is an external and indisputable fact—one that remains absolute regardless of feeling or experience. When our counselees really "know" God's truth, they will change the way they think and make better choices.

2. By Knowing this Truth: Sin's Control over Us has been Destroyed

Knowing this . . . that our body of sin might be done away with [and] that we are no longer slaves to sin.

(Romans 6:6)

Sin has no power over the believer except as his ignorance, unbelief, or passivity to the truth allows it to have control over him. The phrase "done away with" is translated *render powerless* in Hebrews 2:14. Jesus rendered Satan inoperative or powerless when He died on the cross, taking the punishment for all of mankind. It was a legal transaction: Jesus literally stripped Satan of all his power over humanity. This phrase could be paraphrased *I no longer take orders from my body.* Freud's theory of psychology was based on the premise that man is basically a biological being whose physical impulses and urges dictate his choices in life. Not true of the spiritual man: the spiritual man does not take orders from his body anymore!

3. By Considering [Thinking about and Meditating on] the Truth

Even so, consider yourselves to be dead to sin but alive to God in Christ Jesus.

(Romans 6:11)

Before eating fruit from the Tree of the Knowledge of Good and Evil, Adam was "alive" relationally to God and "dead" relationally to sin—and its control over him. After Adam sinned, he died to God and became alive to sin. By His death and resurrection, Jesus restored us to a living and active relationship with God. *Born dead* at the physical birth (Ephesians 2:1), we have been *made alive* by the new birth (Ephesians 2:5).

Paul tells us to *consider* this important truth: we are *dead to sin and alive to God.* The Greek word *consider* derives from the Greek word *legos,* meaning "to say." The word means *to lay, to arrange, to gather or to declare.* The word "consider" means *to declare your thoughts or to set your mind.* It is also an accounting term meaning *to calculate or take into account.* The same word is used in the familiar Philippians 4:8: *Whatever is pure, whatever is lovely . . . let your minds dwell on [consider] these things.* Paul told the Philippians to keep the truth in their minds: think about it, calculate it; add it up, gather it, speak it, declare it. When a believer injects the truth into his every thought, he takes a therapeutic broom and sweeps away the lies and faulty beliefs that have enslaved him. What he speaks—to others and himself—is important too. One's own words carry a power to influence his thinking either to reaffirm or deny the power of the truth. What one tells oneself is crucial to the process of change.

In Romans 4:19, Paul says Abraham *did not consider his own body, already dead.* Although his body was reproductively dead, he did not consider (think about; dwell on; pay attention to) the limitations of his body. The problem with defeated believers is that they are considering their own incapability, liabilities, and disabilities rather than God's truth. An effective Biblical counselor listens to his counselees to discern what it is they are considering—what they are telling themselves.

4. By Making Choices that are Consistent with the Truth

We have seen two conditions for living as though one is *dead to sin and alive to God*: **knowing** and **considering**. Now there is another condition for living in freedom: **choosing**.

> *Therefore, do not let sin reign [be in control] in your mortal body that you should obey its lusts; and do not go on presenting the members of your body to sin as instruments of unrighteousness but present your-selves to God as those alive from the dead . . .*
>
> (Romans 6:12–13)

Paul admonished the believers to **choose** to act on the truth. **Knowing** and **considering** the truth must be followed by **choices** that reflect that truth. Paul exhorts the believer to choose to *present their members* to God as instruments of righteousness. What are *members*? First, "members" refers to the body—one's eyes, ears, speech and all of his physical faculties. Second, *members* refers to one's psychological faculties—thinking, feeling, and acting. God gave these members to man for doing His will. When man aligns his members with God's will, he functions as God intended. In Colossians 3:5, Paul again used the word *members, consider the members of your earthly body as dead to immorality, impurity, passion, evil desire, and greed.* Even more strongly, Paul says, *present your bodies as a living sacrifice* (Romans 12:1). These choices are important; godly choices reinforce the truth experientially. Conversely, wrong choices sabotage one's progress in faith.

There is another noteworthy word in Romans 6:13. The Greek word *instrument* could also be translated *weapon*. This word suggests that one's *members* are like *weapons*; as such they can be used either defensively or offensively. And, as such, they can be used to protect and enhance the believer's relationship with God. Or, members can be used as weapons against his self, in a self-defeating manner.

Summary

Hopefully, we have answered the question "Can I change?" Our affirmative answer is based is based on the great doctrinal statements of Romans 6.

1) We have died with Christ to sin's control.
2) We have received new life and resurrection power.
3) We consider these truths regardless of our feelings.
4) When we act on these truths, we align ourselves with facts, not feelings.

In his book *From Guilt to Glory*, Dr. Ray Stedman sums up the concept of our freedom in Christ and our ability to change with the following words:

> *"We think we have to change the way we act in order to be different, and God says, 'No, I have made you different, and when you believe it, you will automatically change the way you act."*

Diagram 6

THE CROSS OF CHRIST

We *break* the *hold sin* has on
us by relying upon a *new view*
of our self that is true because
we are in Christ Jesus.

*The power of
sin has been
broken
because of our
union in
Christ's death
and
resurrection.*
Romans 6:6

*We are not
to identify
with our
temptations.
We are
not our
temptations.
Feelings
must be
answered by
facts.*

"We think that we have to change the
way we act in order to be different;
God says, No, I have made you
different, and when you believe it
you automatically change the way
you act."
From *Guilt to Glory,* by Ray Stedman

In the next chapter we will answer the question "if these things are true, why is it such a struggle to put them into affect?"

Back to Arthur

Arthur never understood his identity as a "son of God." Continuing to see himself as a son of "his father," he continued to act out that wounded identity. We prayed, asking the Lord to open his eyes to this truth. As Arthur began to comprehend the truth that his "old self" was crucified with Christ, he gained more hope. I asked Arthur to memorize and meditate on Scriptures that contained this truth, especially focusing on Romans 6:11, considering that "Arthur," son of his natural father, who was addicted to sexual sin was "dead" and that a "new" Arthur, son of God, was now alive. Slowly, these truths re-framed Arthur's view of himself. Though there was much work to be done to apply these truths on a daily basis, Arthur had passed through the first obstacle to change. He was no longer in bondage to a wrong view of himself.

QUESTIONS

At our new birth, or regeneration, what happens to the human spirit?

What are some of the things we became at rebirth?

John 1:12_____

2 Corinthians 5:17_____

1 Peter 1:4 _____

In your "old" identity you were the son/daughter of (your father) but in your "new" identity, you are now the son/daughter of _____.

CHAPTER SEVEN

Why is it Such a Struggle?

Scenario:

Marsha was an alcoholic. She grew up in a "good" family: her father was the choir director in her church. Her father never drank in the home but it was his habit to stop at a neighborhood tavern every evening on the way home from work. He would sit quietly in his chair after dinner, hardly interacting with his wife or children. On the weekend's he would visit the local tavern, and return home to more isolation and distance from his family.

Marsha grew up a rebellious child, acting out the family dysfunction in her own life. But Marsha was not a "quiet drunk." When she drank she became loud and offensive. By the time she came to see me, she was a divorced 30-year old woman with a son in grade school. She was still struggling with her alcohol addiction, even after having been in recovery groups for several years. As she explained her struggle to me, she said: "I don't know how I can be a Christian and still be drinking out of control all the time. Maybe I'm not really born again." When I questioned her further, she said she had asked Christ to come in to her heart several times, and in her view, to no avail!

It was clear that Marsha did not understand her identity in Christ, but also that she did not understand the "struggle" all believers must go through as they "crucify the flesh," achieve victory, and walk in the Spirit.

All believers experience this tension. Fleshly desires create an opposition in the soul to the things of the Spirit. Paul expresses this idea in his letters; the following two verses especially show the depth of the struggle.

The flesh sets its desire against the Spirit and the Spirit against the flesh; for these are in opposition to one another; so that you may not do the things that you please . . . For I know that nothing good dwells in me, that is, in my flesh; for the willing is present in me, but the doing of the good is not.

(Galatians 5:17; Romans 7:18)

As we have stated in the earlier chapters, when one is born again, he has a radical identity change: he is no longer an *in the flesh* person; he is an *in the Spirit* person (Romans 8:9). However, a believer can continue to live under the control of his flesh. But when he does, he is not expressing his spiritual identity, the *new self*. He is expressing the identity of his *old self*, also referred to by Paul as one's *former manner of life* (Ephesians 4:22).

In this chapter we will answer the questions: Why is it difficult to change? What is the flesh? What does it mean to crucify the flesh? These questions are answered under the rubric of the doctrine of sanctification.

WHAT IS THE FLESH?

And I, brethren, could not speak to you as to spiritual men, but as to men of flesh, as to infants in Christ. I gave you milk to drink, not solid food; for you were not yet able to receive it. Indeed, even now you are not yet able, for you are still fleshly .

(1 Corinthians 3:1–3)

In these verses, Paul defines *flesh* in two ways to enlighten our understanding.

1. Prolonged Spiritual Immaturity

First, Paul defines flesh as *spiritual immaturity: I could not speak to you as to spiritual men but as to men of flesh, as to babies in Christ.* When one is first born again, he may look more like a *natural* man than a *spiritual* man—a **man of flesh** or **like flesh**—after all, he is baby Christian. But he is supposed to grow. People who do not grow after their new birth are like spiritual toddlers—they have not yet learned the appropriate controls over their body, mind, and emotions. The people in the Corinth church were spiritually immature. Paul was unable to dialogue with them as *adults* in the Lord. (Have you ever tried to have an intelligent and stimulating conversation with a toddler?) Each believer begins his Christian life as an infant. Then God calls him to "grow up." Just as a parent does not give in to a child's whines and demands to have his own way, the soul is like a spoiled child who needs to be stripped of its self-centeredness and stubbornness to make everyone conform to its way! The Psalmist expresses it this way: *Like a weaned child rests against his mother, my soul is like a weaned child within me* (Psalm 131:2). Paul too recognizes this principle: *When I was a child, I spoke as a child, I understood as a child, I thought as a child: but when I became a man, I put away childish things* (1 Corinthians 13:11). Believers who have not appropriately matured are fleshly.

2. Controlled by Natural Desires

A second feature of flesh is explained in Paul's phrase *you are still fleshly* (verse 3). The Greek word means *under the control of the flesh.*

When believers do not progress, they regress, and their fleshly desires control them. In Roman 7:23, Paul says that indwelling sin (our flesh) attempts to bring us into captivity, *making me a prisoner of the law of sin which is in my members*. Peter also exhorts the believers to *abstain from fleshly lusts which wage war against the soul* (1 Peter 2:11). Then in Romans 8:12–13, Paul declares *we are no longer under obligation to the flesh, to live according to the flesh*, then promises *if by the Spirit you are putting to death the deeds of the flesh, you will live*. Paul exhorts the believers not to be controlled by the flesh, but to exercise the power and authority inherent within them by way of their new birth (see chapter 6). Believers who are controlled by their natural desires are fleshly.

THE "FLESHLY" PERSON MEETS HIS NEEDS BY SELF-EFFORT

God intended that our needs would be fulfilled in relationship with Him. When we do not allow God to meet our needs, there is a vacuum—these vacuums need to be filled (see Diagram 7). Every natural man has them. These vacuums turn him to fleshly indulgences, immediate gratifications, and anything that feels good. What we call *flesh*, then, is simply one's self-centered and sense-oriented method of trying to fill up that emptiness (see definitions of flesh in diagram 7).

But living *in the flesh* is stressful and burdensome. It produces anger, anxiety, and depression. The work of the flesh (self-effort) keeps the believer earthbound and weak. Christians who live this way feel unsure of their salvation—they are unable to reconcile their daily struggle with their professed faith in the power of Jesus.

WALKING A NEW WAY: THE PURPOSE OF BIBLICAL COUNSELING

*But I say, **walk** by the Spirit and you will not carry out the desires of the flesh.*

(Galatians 5:16)

To illustrate this spiritual concept, I would like to share a spiritual insight I gained from my parenting experience: watching my child "learning to walk!" Our daughter Esther was a cautious child, so she reluctantly approached this new task. By the time she was a full year old, we were able to coax her into taking her first serious steps. Oh, how warily her mother and I guided her through these first attempts! But with time and practice her walk became more confident. Along with confidence, however, she became careless of the hidden dangers that more experienced "walkers" are aware of. Then one day it happened! On our vacation in a rural California town, she stumbled over an unruly plank in the boardwalk. She tumbled headfirst, skinning her forehead as well as her knees. I was struck with the horrible guilt parents feel when they have failed to protect their child from some unseen danger. Thank God children are resilient! Even after that accident, Esther never retreated. Each time she tripped or fell, she would pick herself up (perhaps her mother or I picked her up!) and walk again. Though in time I grew to be less fearful for her, I did catch myself feeling anxious whenever she would walk on a trail filled with ruts or on a sidewalk etched with canyon-sized cracks. There were always opportunities for stumbling, but Esther learned to avoid them. She learned to walk.

I began with this story to illustrate just how much effort is involved in something as mundane as walking. Imagine what it would be like if you woke up one morning and couldn't remember how to walk! How would you go about starting to learn all over again? From those extraordinary persons who have ever had to relearn to walk as adults, for whatever reason, I am sure we could learn a lot about the endurance and hard work it takes.

In the spiritual realm, we learn to walk too. Helping people to *walk* is an essential part of Biblical counseling. Diagnosing the problem, and even developing a treatment plan, is easy by comparison. The hard part is assisting the counselee to *walk* it. Why? Because he has been walking the *old* way for so long, it feels impossible to learn a new walk. It has been referred to as the *tyranny of the familiar*.

Paul likens the entirety of the Christian life to the process of learning to walk. The analogy of walking is an appropriate one. Just as we learned to walk in the natural world, we learn to walk in the spiritual world. Anyone who has ever tried to change an old habit for a new one knows that it is a demanding process of successes and failures. And just as God has instilled basic instincts that motivate psychological and physical growth, He has instilled in His spiritual children a desire for spiritual growth. No matter how many times we stumble, we just keep getting up again!

WALKING IN THE SPIRIT MEANS "CRUCIFYING THE FLESH"

In his letter to the Galatians, Paul develops his *walking* theme— *walking in the Spirit* requires *crucifying the flesh*. We must be sure our counselees understand this important process that every believer must go through. The following passage identifies four basic steps of learning to walk in the Spirit and crucify the flesh.

> But I say, walk by the Spirit and you will not carry out the desire of the flesh . . . *those who belong to Christ Jesus have crucified the flesh with its passions and desires. Since we live in the Spirit, let us also walk by the Spirit.*
>
> (Galatians 5:16, 24–25)

Step One: We must deliberately commit to walk by the Spirit (v. 16, 25)

Counseling begins with a commitment to *walk by the Spirit*. In Paul's writings, there is a recurring theme: there are two mutually exclusive principles: walking by the Spirit or living in the flesh. Obviously, one cannot do both at the same time. Every believer acknowledges that when he has committed a sin, by giving into his fleshly desires, he was not walking by the Spirit. The solution to the problem of fleshliness is so simple: **walk by the Spirit!** In his letter to the Ephesians, Paul taught using the theme of walking: 1) walk worthy; 2) walk humbly; 3) walk in unity, 4) walk differently (than nonbelievers); 5) walk in love; 6) walk in light; and 7) walk in wisdom.

Note: The word most frequently used in the New Testament for *walk* is the Greek word *parapateo*. This word means: *to walk around*, and is used figuratively by Paul to mean *to conduct oneself in a certain manner*. The word suggests progress. To walk is to proceed; it is both active and progressive.

Step Two: We must prepare for a struggle (v. 17)

It is essential that we alert our counselees that their goal to *walk by the Spirit* will be opposed by strong fleshly desires. Whenever a believer makes a commitment to *walk by the Spirit*, he can expect his flesh to be resistant. The flesh has been programmed from childhood to meet one's needs. Growing up in a sinful world, everyone has learned to meet his needs sinfully independent of God. But this fleshly way is an offense to God—it must die: flesh and spirit cannot co-exist. There can be no compromise; "détente" is not an option!

Paul says we have "weapons" to fight the flesh (2 Corinthians 10:5). These weapons are *divinely powerful for the destruction of strongholds*. These *strongholds* are fleshly mental structures of deceptive and faulty thinking. The believer will engage in this battle of the mind every time he attempts to walk in the Spirit.

In Peter's writings, he reminds the believers to expect suffering. He exhorts them to *abstain from fleshly lusts which wage war against the soul* (1 Peter 2:11) and *to arm themselves for the same purpose [as Christ] for he who has suffered in the flesh has ceased from sin* (1 Peter 4:1). Denying one's fleshly urges will result in pain and suffering. The Biblical counselor does a disservice to his counselee if he does not prepare him for this struggle. Too many believers have bought the lie that the walk of faith should not be so difficult.

Step Three: We must crucify the flesh with its passions and desires (v. 24)

We must teach our counselees what it means to *crucify the flesh*. The flesh cannot be tamed, trained, or lamed. It must be killed! Paul says: *I carry about in my body the dying of Jesus in order that the life of Jesus may be manifested in my mortal flesh . . . for I have been crucified with Christ.* Then Paul declares the ultimate goal of our death: *it is no longer I who live, but Christ lives in me* (2 Corinthians 4:10; Galatians 2:20).

Crucifying the flesh involves a process of thinking differently and choosing differently. There is an identifiable process involved in crucifying the flesh (see diagram 8); the following four steps show that process.

1. When there is some emotional stimulus, feeling of emptiness and deficit, I must acknowledge that these feelings emanate from my fleshly desires to meet my needs.

2. Because I cannot change my feelings, I must identify the wrong thinking that underlies the negative feelings (what am I telling myself to cause these feelings?)

3. During the process I must choose Godly behaviors regardless of my feelings. Thus, I *crucify* those feelings by **not** giving attention to them—death by neglect!

4. I must take all thoughts captive to the obedience of Christ and allow God to renew my mind, setting my mind on things above, believing God will meet my need in the moment.

The Metaphor of *Putting off* and *Putting on*

In reference to your former manner of life you lay aside the old self which is being corrupted in accordance with the lusts of deceit and that you be renewed in the spirit of your mind and put on the new self, which in the likeness of God has been created in righteousness and holiness of the truth.

(Ephesians 4:22–24)

This metaphor is so helpful to Biblical counselors to explain what it means to *crucify the flesh*. It is the metaphor *putting off* and *putting on*. *Putting off the old self* requires: 1) identifying one's fleshly strategies, goal-oriented behaviors (you cannot put off what you don't know about!) and 2) stopping wrong behavior.

Put them all aside: anger, wrath, malice, slander, and abusive speech from your mouth.

(Colossians 3:8)

Conversely, *putting on the new self* requires both renewing the mind and choosing Godly behaviors. Behaviors are directly related to the "old" belief system—what a person tells himself he needs to do in order to meet his needs. Paul explains this dual process:

1. Renewing the mind

> *Consider the members of your earthly body as dead to immorality, impurity, passion, evil desire, and greed, which amount to idolatry.*
>
> (Colossians 3:5)

2. Choosing godly behaviors

> *Present your members to God . . . Practice these things.*
>
> (Romans 6:13; Philippians 4:9)

As a person *puts off the old self*—behaviorally—and is renewed in his thinking, he will *put on the new self.* His flesh no longer controls him; his walk will become consistent and steady in that area of his life. He has *crucified the flesh with its passions and desires.* He is *living in the Spirit* and *walking by the Spirit.*

Step Four: Practice walking *by the Spirit* (v. 25)

Biblical counselors are able to provide hope to their counselees that eventually they will arrive at their destination: a new walk by the Spirit. As each of us grows and matures as God's *sons,* our walk will become a standard by which we live. It is a strong and confident stride with the Holy Spirit—more sensitive, cooperative, teachable, and humble; we are less likely to stumble so badly. The Old Testament prophet Habakkuk spoke eloquently of this *walk* long before Paul: *The Lord God is my strength, and He has made my feel like hinds' feet and makes me walk on my high places* (Habakkuk 3:19), signifying sure-footed confidence. This is the power of resurrection life we receive upon new birth *in order that the life of Jesus may be manifested in [our] mortal flesh.* Without this resurrection power, no believer can expect to make progress. In his book *The Ultimate Intention,* DeVern Fromke puts it so well: *With men (who rely on their own re-*

sources) these things are impossible, but for those who are in union with God all things are possible—HIM possible.

Note: The word for **walk** used in verse 25 is not the same Greek word used in verse 16. The Greek word is *stoixeo.* Used only five times in Paul's letters, it means "to frame one's conduct by a certain rule." The connotation is of a "regimented" walk of soldiers, marching in lock-step with one another. In Philippians 3:16, *stoixeo* is translated "standard." *Let us therefore as many as are perfect [mature] have this attitude . . . let us keep living by that same **standard** to which we have attained.* This word surely indicates that one's walk becomes more consistent and steady after one has *crucified the flesh with its passions and desires.*

How Long Will It Take?

Would it be correct to say the struggle will never be over while we live in these mortal bodies? Yes. But it would be just as correct to say that the struggle is not the normal Christian life. Struggles are episodic; they have a beginning and an end. But we must be careful to cooperate with the Lord's process. Each time we struggle to crucify our fleshly strategies, if we resist His work in us, it will last longer than it needs to. (It usually takes longer than we are willing to accept because the *issues* are deeper than we thought.)

The internal work of God is what we call transformation, meaning to change from the inside. An effective Biblical counselor will teach his counselee that the struggle between the Spirit and the flesh results in transformation. Praise God, by the struggle the believer is *conformed* to the image of Christ: *put on the new self, which in the likeness of God has been created in righteousness and holiness of the truth* (Ephesians 4:22–24).

THE ULTIMATE PURPOSE OF SANCTIFICATION

God's first call to man (through Adam) was to rule over the earth. His last call (through Christ) is to reign with Him on high. Living the enthroned Christian life is one of glory and satisfaction. But this life requires sacrifice. Our Father has allowed us the privilege of entering into the sufferings and discipline of Christ that we might fulfill His desire to *bring many sons to glory* (Hebrews 4:10). If we endure, we will reign with Him (2 Timothy 2:12). This is certainly the abundant life that Jesus promised to those who would pick up their cross and follow Him.

Back to Marsha

Marsha began to distinguish between her feelings and her thoughts. She began to comprehend the truth that her flesh was not her identity. And most importantly, Marsha began to accept that truth that "new life" in Christ was both a "proclamation" and a "process." She had been influenced by her culture and by wrong doctrine to assume that life in Christ was supposed to be easy and comfortable. Understand-

Diagram 7

WHAT IS FLESH?

"The flesh is a built-in law of failure, making it impossible for natural man to please or serve God. It is a compulsive inner force inherited from man's fall, which expresses itself in general and specific rebellion against God and His righteousness. The flesh can never be reformed or improved. The only hope for escape from the law of the flesh is its total execution and replacement by a new life in the Lord Jesus Christ. This terrible force is within us, and even after we have by faith counted him dead, he will attempt to spring to life again and control us."   Mark Bubeck, *The Adversary*

"Flesh is the urge to self-centeredness within us, that distortion of human nature which makes us want to be our own god—that proud ego, that uncrucified self which is the seat of willful defiance and rebellion against authority."   Ray Stedman, *Spiritual Warfare*

"The flesh is man as he has allowed himself to become in contrast with man as God meant him to be. The flesh stands for human nature, weakened, vitiated, tainted by sin. The flesh is man as he is apart from Jesus Christ and his Spirit."   William Barclay, *Flesh and Spirit*

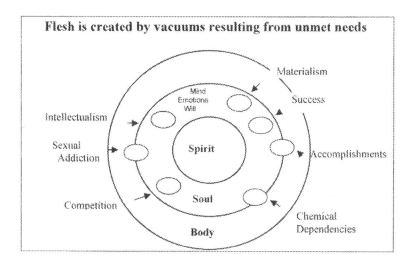

Diagram 8

CRUCIFYING THE FLESH

Flesh Reality
Death

↑

Because the fleshly
strategy does not satisfy,
negative feelings result
and the cycle starts over

↑

Pain is temporarily
relieved by one's
flesh strategy

↑

Pain motivates a
person to meet his
needs

↑

The consequence is pain:
I do not belong; I am
not loved; I do not
matter

↑

The Response is passive:
feelings take over

↑

There is an emotional
stimulus that
demands a response:
angry, anxious,
depressed

Faith Reality
Life

↑

Expect to
experience
fruit and joy
of the Spirit

↑

Take thoughts
captive to the
obedience of Christ

↑

Deny the fleshly
emotion by not
paying attention to it

↑

Make a commitment
to Godly choices

↑

Identify wrong
thoughts and deal with
appropriately

↑

Recognize
feelings are
as fleshly

ing the "struggle" and recognizing the reality of "spiritual warfare" allowed Marsha to abide in Christ in a way she had never known before. She picked up her armor and began a warfare lifestyle of crucifying her flesh.

QUESTIONS

In Galatians 5:17, what are the two opponents?

How does Ray Stedman define "flesh?"

After regeneration, what happens to the human soul? (see Romans12:2)

How does Paul describe crucifying the flesh in Ephesians 4:22–24 (there are three steps)?

What does Paul tell us will happen when we suffer in the flesh (2 Peter 4:1)?

CHAPTER EIGHT

Making Better Choices

Scenario:

Bob, a man in his late 20's, married eight years, was referred to me for marriage counseling. He and his wife were having tremendous conflict in their marriage; she was considering divorce. As I talked with Bob I learned the following: his wife had just discovered that he had been having an "emotional" affair with a woman at work. Bob seemed totally unrepentant. He justified his actions by telling me that his wife Nancy had been very unhappy in their marriage. Her constant complaining was such a source of anxiety and stress for Bob that he had sought emotional comfort outside of the marriage.

I asked Bob to tell me more about these eight years of marriage. I learned that Bob had averaged over fifty hours a week at work over the last several years and had been attending college at night. The weekends were filled up with studying and it left little time for his wife and two young children. Nancy had been left to do all the child rearing and family responsibilities alone. When I asked Bob why he had chosen to spend so little time with his wife and children, he responded with surprise: "I didn't choose to be away from home so much. My job and my schooling required it of me." Bob could not at first see that doing these things was a choice. And by doing them, he was choosing not to spend time with his family. Bob knew how to be a student; he knew how to work hard. Bob, however, felt very inadequate for the role of husband and father. The way Bob viewed himself correlated to the choices he was making.

As I got to know Bob better, I learned that his own mother was very controlling and critical. Bob had never learned how to view Nancy apart from his mother. Hence, Nancy's attempts to get Bob's attention were interpreted by Bob as control and criticism. By his choices, Bob was distancing himself from Nancy. And the choices he made confirmed Bob's belief that he would never be a good husband or father.

CHARACTER AND CHOICES

In the previous chapters, we have emphasized the importance of a proper mindset. A commitment to the truth and right thinking produces faith. However, faith is not just agreement with a truth; faith must be put to action. So now we must also consider the importance of the "will," the volitional piece of Biblical counseling.

James says *faith without works is a dead faith* (James 2:26). These "works"—our behaviors—are the outward expression of our inner life. And our behaviors are the result of our choices. And one's choices must be consistent with one's commitment to the truth: the believer's *walk* must demonstrate his faith! Therefore, the Biblical counselor must pay attention to his counselee's choices. Why?

1. Choices reveal one's character

For the purpose of this teaching, let us define character as self-image and self-esteem. The way we view ourselves and the way we feel about ourselves determines what kind of choices we will make.

Where your treasure is [the things that are important to us are the things we choose] there will your heart be also (Matthew 6:21).

2. Choices determine one's character

Jesus said, *But those things which proceed out of the mouth come forth from the heart; and they defile the man* (Matthew 15:18). By each thought and choice we are building our character. Either we are building a character that will last through eternity or one that will be worthless. *But let each man be careful how he builds* (1 Corinthians 1:30).

A LIFE THAT IS *SINCERE AND BLAMELESS* IS THE RESULT
OF MAKING BETTER CHOICES
APPROVING THE THINGS THAT ARE EXCELLENT MEANS
OBEDIENCE

Changing behavior is an obvious goal of counseling. Every counselee has some sinful behavior that is sabotaging his spiritual and psychological progress. These problem behaviors drive a person to the counseling office. The counselee desires, in a word, to be **obedient**. Obedience is the result of the life of true faith. Paul told the Roman Christians he was please that they were *obedient from the heart* (Romans 6:17). Many believers do not recognize that their spiritual impotence is a result of poor choices. Therefore, we should give attention to this important component of Biblical counseling: helping the counselee to make better choices.

Paul's prayer to the Philippians provides us with his insight on what it takes to make good choices. Paul says the **love, real knowledge**, and **discernment** will result in **better choices**, *approving the things that are excellent,* producing a Christian whose walk is pure and blameless.

> *And this I pray that your **love** may abound still more and more in real knowledge and all discernment so that you may approve the things that are excellent in order to be sincere and blameless . . .*
>
> (Philippians 1:9–10)

ABOUNDING LOVE

1. As a Motivator for Change

Not surprisingly, Paul prays for their love to increase in order to enlarge their capacity for knowing God and discerning His will. Love is a powerful motivation for obedience. Jesus said *if you truly love me you will keep my commandments* (John 14:23). Love is the most powerful force at work in the world. John puts it quite simply: *God is*

Love (1 John 4:8). Jesus declares the Father's love for fallen man: *God so loved the world that He gave His only begotten son* (John 3:16). Our response to love is to want to please the one who loves us: *we love because He first loved us* (1 John 4:19). Love is the motivation for making better choices.

Often a counselee's love relationship with the Lord is quite deficient. Therefore, his motivation is weak. This produces a condition called ambivalence and the counselee will be resistant to change. When a counselee's motivation is weak, pray with him; ask for the Spirit's motivation. The psalmist says to *delight yourself in the Lord, and He will give you the desires of your heart* (Psalm 37:4).

NOTE: In my marriage counseling practice, I assess each partner's motivation level. Before making a commitment to work with them, I need to know how committed they are to their marriage and to the counseling process. I know that our progress will be sabotaged by a reluctant partner. It is not unusual for a one partner to attend marriage counseling for the sake of appearance. That is to say, he or she is already planning to leave the marriage, but wants to appear as though they really tried. Wisdom says to discern the level of motivation before proceeding.

2. As a Motivator for Enduring Suffering

Another reason Paul prays for increased love is so that believers will be able to endure the suffering that is necessary to make better choices. As recorded in Luke 14:28–32, Jesus told His disciples two parables about *counting the cost*. In the first parable Jesus spoke of a man who builds a tower: *Who will not count the cost to see if he has enough to finish?* The second concerned a king who went out to do battle and met a king coming against him with a powerful army. Jesus said: *What king, when he sets out to meet another king in battle, will not first sit down and consider whether he is strong enough with ten thousand men to encounter the one coming against him with twenty thousand?*

The Lord is saying to us: "If you are going to become a Christian, you should think it through. You should count the cost of discipleship. You should see if you really mean business and are going to carry this through." He says it is foolish to start on a course of action if we have not first figured how much we will need to finish. Notice that Jesus precedes these illustrations with His words: *Whoever does not carry his own cross and come after me cannot be my disciple.* Has your counselee considered what that will mean for him? Does it mean he may have to give up some friends or a relationship? Will it mean a move, or a change of jobs, or a new church? It will certainly mean he will have to give up control over his life. The Lord is looking for such to be His followers.

When I returned to the Lord after my *prodigal* period of a dozen years, I had to change a lot of bad habits; it was very difficult. The Lord gave me a passage that encouraged me. Some might read it and wonder how I could be encouraged by a passage on suffering. But to me, it was a very simple statement showing how I would be able to change. This passage became my "anchor" during times I was tempted to return to my old behaviors.

Therefore, since Christ has suffered in the flesh, arm yourselves also with the same purpose; because he who has suffered in the flesh has ceased from sin.

(1 Peter 4:1)

The answer is so simple it can escape us. If we are willing to suffer the pain of saying no to sin, the habits will die. More precisely, if we have a habit that is hard to break, the more we stop doing it, the more it will hurt. And the more we hurt from not doing it, the closer we get to breaking that habit. All we need to do is suffer. A counselee needs to understand this principle: if he continues in sinful habits, he will suffer the consequences of the sinful act itself. Ever since the Fall, man has tried to persuade himself he will not reap what he sows!

In another passage, Peter says: *by no means let any of you suffer as a murder, or thief, or evildoer, or a troublesome meddler; but if anyone suffers as a Christian, let him not feel ashamed, but in that name let him glorify God* (1 Pet 4:15–16). The Biblical counselor must discern if his counselee has considered what it may cost him to change. And he must prepare his counselee to suffer for making the right choices.

Real Knowledge

1. A Changed Mind

A person cannot truly *change his behavior* until he has had a *change of mind*. We now must consider this: the objective of Biblical counseling is to bring about a change of mind, i.e., to dispel ignorance. The Biblical counselor will discern what truth his counselee needs to "know" in order to bring about a spiritual alignment. As long as a counselee remains ignorant of God's truth, Satan has an advantage over him (2 Corinthians 2:11). Likewise, as long as a counselee remains ignorant of fleshly strategies, Satan has an advantage over him. St. Augustine prayed to God, *Let me know myself, Lord, and I will know you.* David said, *Search me, O God, and know my heart . . . see if there is any hurtful way in me* (Psalm 139:23–24). The one who is more knowledgeable always has an advantage over the one who is ignorant. One of Satan's primary objectives is to keep believers in darkness, blind to the truth of God: *. . . the god of this world has blinded the minds of the unbelieving that they might not see the light . . .* (2 Corinthians 4:4).

2. An Enlightened Mind

In this prayer for the Philippians (1:9–10), Paul asks God to give them *real knowledge*. Paul prayed similarly for the Ephesians:

> *. . . that the God of our Lord Jesus Christ . . . may give to you a spirit of wisdom and of **revelation** in the knowledge of Him . . . that the eyes of your heart may be **enlightened**, so that you may **know** what is the hope of His calling, what are the riches of the glory of His inheritance in the saints, and what is the surpassing greatness of His power toward us who believe .*
>
> (Ephesians1:17–20)

Paul knew they needed enlightenment that could only happen by way of revelation by the Holy Spirit if they were going to make the best choices. Many counselees will say they "know" God's truths but the fruit of their lives reveals that truth has not become *real*. Jesus said, *you shall **know** the truth and the truth will set you free* (John 8:12).

3. A Renewed Mind

Paul assured the believers if their minds were renewed, they would *know* God's perfect will in any situation. *Be transformed by the renewing of your mind so that you may prove what the good and acceptable and perfect will of God is* (Romans 12:2). A man whose mind has been renewed by the knowledge of God's Word will make no mistake concerning the will of God. Better choices are not possible without a renewing of the mind. Furthermore, a man whose mind is enlightened and renewed will see all things as they relate to God's perspective.

4. A Protected Mind

Negative thought patterns and habits continually defeat a person. These negative thought patterns are the "enemies" every believer faces in the battle of the mind (2 Corinthians 10:5). Sometimes it is easy to identify enemy thoughts but other times these thoughts are disguised in rationalization. Believers must carefully examine their thoughts to align them with God's truth. Once a believer has identified a thought as an *intruder*, he must be quick to deal with that thought before it leads to a wrong attitude or action. Although he may have convinced himself otherwise, he can control his thoughts. Paul states this very clearly when he says, *we are taking every thought captive to the obedience of Christ* (2 Corinthians 10:5). In the Garden of Gethsemane Jesus said to His disciples, *Keep watching and praying that you may not enter into temptation.* (Mat 26:39). This Greek word "watch" is also used by Peter in the closing remarks of his first letter (5:8), when he says, be *of sober spirit; be on the* **alert**.

5. An Occupied Mind

Negative thoughts need to be displaced (*put off and put on*— Ephesians 4:22–24). One cannot stop thinking a negative thought without replacing it with a positive one. Otherwise, he is left with a void in his thinking. He is "empty-headed!" Paul declares this concept of thought displacement with these words, *Finally, brethren, whatever is true, whatever is honorable, whatever is right, whatever is of good repute, if there is any excellence and if anything is worthy of praise, let your mind dwell on these things* (Philippians 4:8).

ALL DISCERNMENT

Discernment is the ability to distinguish God's thoughts and ways from all others. It is the ability to differentiate one's own *natural* thoughts and motives from those of the Spirit. Because there are so many choices these days and because we are living in a time of such moral relativity, we pray, as Paul did, that believers develop the faculty of spiritual discernment that they might avoid many problems. The Holy Spirit enables the believer by way of "discernment" to make better choices.

Note: *Discernment* correlates with *real knowledge*, suggesting that discernment results from a fuller knowledge of Scripture and of God as a Person. The root of the word *discernment* implies "a sense of taste." One who has had his *spiritual taste buds* trained can detect the slightest difference between flavors.

As believers *walk* by the Spirit, each step necessitates making finer distinctions between "things that differ." The further we go, the sharper these distinctions must become. Paul assures the believers that the one who has developed this *capacity* of discernment will make better choices.

Discernment will result in wiser choices

By growing in discernment, believers begin to see they are making poor choices in things they take for granted. They do not realize how many things in their daily lifestyle may be affecting them adversely. Moses taught the Israelites that a godly lifestyle ought to be integrated into one's daily schedule (Deuteronomy 6: 5–9). One's daily choices will either sabotage or support his progress. Anyone who is serious about change will want to examine his daily routine. Does it support the life to which God is calling him? If he wants to arise earlier in the morning to have quality Bible study and prayer time, he needs to plan an early bedtime the night before. The activities one does with his discretionary time (television, reading, hobbies, and social life) require scrutiny in this light. Do they support the changes he wants to make? The counselee must ask himself "do the choices in my daily routine support my goals?" The Biblical counselor should help the counselee to see if he is making poor choices though his daily lifestyle. This includes helping him to see if he is putting himself in the place of greatest opportunity for growth. A mature believer will expose himself to God's opportunities and associate with His people.

> Note: *Once I was counseling a young man who was struggling with sexual addiction. The places for many such men used to be the many "adult bookstores" or porno shops around our cities (now men can find such things to fill their appetite right in their homes via the internet). One of the first things he and I agreed upon is that he would make every effort to avoid these adult bookstores. Instead, he was to plan his free time carefully and cultivate good, healthy, accountable relationships with men at his church. One day, as he was leaving my office, he told me that there were no less than five adult bookstores on the route between my office and his home. He said that as he passed each one, he was tempted to stop and go in. I asked him if he had ever considered going a different way home so that he did not have to pass any of these places. He seemed surprised at such a simple remedy to the problem of temptation.*

SINCERE AND BLAMELESS

1. Open, Genuine, Humble

The word *sincere* means "purity which has withstood the test." The literal translation of the word *sincere*, in Latin, means "without wax." The origin of this word dates back to the Roman period when having marble statues in the home was as common as houseplants. If a sculptor's creation was made from deficient marble, there might be cracks in the finished work. In order to cover the cracks, the less scrupulous artist would fill them in with transparent wax. Upon placing the statue in the sunlight, the wax would melt and the cracks would show through. At some time in a believer's life every crack in his structure that has been concealed will become apparent. These are indicators that his choices have **not** been "excellent."

2. A Steady, Consistent Walk

The word *blameless* brings us back to the metaphor of *walking*. It means "not to **stumble** or jar against the moral rule." It comes from a root word meaning "keeping an eye out." This word incorporates many of the ideas we have already discussed: watching and praying; reading and meditating on God's Word as our standard; looking for the "cracks" in our life. It does not mean "sinless" for that would be contrary to Scripture (1 John 1:8). The blameless man is one who consistently desires to do what is right and have his imperfections removed.

A FINAL WORD ABOUT CHANGING BEHAVIORS

Paul's prayer in Philippians 1:9–10 is not a prayer for greater will power. Paul does not place emphasis on making changes. His emphasis is clearly on growing in love, knowledge, and discernment **so that** the believers would "approve the things that are excellent," making better choices. In the letter to the Ephesians (5:18) Paul exhorts the believer to be *[continually] filled with the Spirit.* Without submission to the Holy Spirit, for His power, the believer is just relying on his own will power. God has a higher way. He Himself has made provision for us through the infilling of His Spirit. God Himself gives the believer the ability to do that which is *pleasing in His sight* (1 John 3:22), *for it is God who is at work in you, both to will and to work for His good pleasure* (Philippians 2:13).

QUESTIONS

What are the two reasons choices are important?

What are the three keys necessary to make better choices?

What is "revelation knowledge?" How is it different from intellectual knowledge?

If you were counseling someone who was trying to change a long-standing habit, how would you prepare him/her for "counting the cost?"

CHAPTER NINE

Feelings: What Good are they?

Scenario:

Alice was referred to counseling by her pastor for problem with anger. Alice had been married for seven years. She had two children: one still in diapers, the other 5 years old. She was increasingly acting out her anger with her children. She told me that she had been yelling a lot and saying things to them she knew were not good for their self-esteem. She was unable to keep the house as nice as she used to. Between taking her little boy to soccer practices and games and caring for her toddler, she could not find time for herself: she felt like things were spinning out of control. In a recent event that led to her seeking professional help, her son spilled his milk one morning and she spanked him, yelling at him to the point she felt out of control. She felt guilty about it. She confessed that she hated feeling inadequate; she especially didn't like feeling so angry all the time. And she hated the fact that she was feeling out of control. And Alice was quickly succumbing to a feeling of depression. By way of some probing, I learned her parents had been un-affirming and had high expectations of her.

Unwanted, undesirable feelings are the reason people seek counseling. They are experiencing some form of **anxiety, depression, or anger**. An effective Biblical counselor knows how to use a counselee's "feelings" diagnostically, that is, to understand the problem. There is much confusion about the role of feelings in Biblical counseling. Most Christians have a strong expectation—rightly or not—that "regeneration" (new birth) should make them "feel" better. Unfortunately, there is confusion about the role of "feelings" in Biblical counseling. Is it only about changing behavior? Do feelings matter? Certainly, no one will argue that behavior—in a word, obedience—is vital to one's psychological and spiritual growth. But the counselor must be able to answer his counselee's questions: "Why do I feel angry?" "Why do I feel anxious?" "Why do I feel depressed?"

The purpose of this chapter is to help the Biblical counselor understand the significance of "negative" or "problem" feelings for the counselee. (I will define these negative feelings as those that make us uncomfortable, unhappy, or guilty.) Let us compare *negative* feelings to the warning lights on the dashboard of a car. When there is something wrong in the engine, those red lights turn on or flash. All cars have a warning light that tells the driver when his fuel tank is almost empty (new cars even have an auto attendant voice that may speak to the driver!). Isn't it ironic that when people are tired or hungry it is like feeling empty? And when empty, they are more emotionally vulnerable. In the same way, there *is* a correlation between the mind (the engine) and the feelings (the warning lights). Problem feelings, like warning lights, indicate problem thinking—thus, the Biblical emphasis on renewing the mind with God's truth (Romans 12:2; Philippians 4:9).

The chart at the end of the chapter shows the relationship between thoughts, behaviors and negative feelings. Please refer to diagram 9 as I explain the progressive development of a person's beliefs and values, the corresponding behaviors (choices), and consequent emotional responses. To be concise, a person's **feelings** tell him what he **believes** he needs to **do** to *meet his needs*.

In the Beginning

Scripture shows that God designed man to need Him (see chapter 5); thus, Adam had the need to belong, to be loved unconditionally, and to matter. Ever since the Fall of mankind—and the resulting separation from God—every child is born into a stressful world that cannot possibly meet his needs. This stress produces a basic anxiety. And no family, however healthy, can completely meet the child's needs and allay that feeling of anxiety. [By the way, this was the first feeling that Adam experienced after he sinned. God says, "why are you hiding?" and Adam responds, "because I was afraid."] This primal feeling is the universal fear of inadequacy that says, "I am not good enough; I am needy." And in a very primal sense, a child will begin seeking answers to the questions:

"Do I belong? Am I loved? Do I matter?"

Developing a Belief System

In the formative years, a child develops his cognitive and intellectual abilities: he is learning. In the stage of cognitive development, a child builds his belief structures. In so doing, he is answering these questions about himself. During this growth period, the child's self-image and self-esteem—how he views himself and what he thinks about himself—are established. Significantly, a person's belief system is developed during childhood when his rational skills are very limited. Accordingly, he is vulnerable to distortions and exaggerated feelings. Even so, these perceptions will have a huge influence on him for the rest of his life. They remain the dominant force of his life until they are recognized and deliberately changed. The need to be deliberate about changing these influences is confirmed in Paul's writings: *when I was a child I thought as a child . . . but when I became a man, I put away childish things* (1 Corinthians 13:11). Paul acknowledges that a person's thinking is formed by his culture and upbringing. Therefore, in several of Paul's letters (Romans 12:2, Ephesians 4:22–24; Colossians 3:9; Titus 3:5), he exhorts the believers that if they are going to *put off the old self* they must be *renewed* in their thinking. Thus, he says, *do not be conformed to this world [these influences], but be transformed by the renewing of your mind.*

Developing Goal-Oriented Behaviors

In early years, a child develops volitionally. Whether a child is strong-willed or passive becomes apparent by the time he is two years old. In the volitional stage of development, the child develops **behaviors** that result from his **beliefs**—what he believes he needs to do to meet his needs. If he tells himself "I do not belong" or "I do not matter," and therefore believes that "people are not safe," he may *believe* (tell himself) "I must NOT get close to people or they will hurt me." His behaviors will reflect that belief; he will maintain distance from others. Or if a young girl says "I must have many friends in order to feel like I belong," she will choose popularity at all costs. Nothing is more important than making friends. Her survival depends on it. These behaviors are her attempts to meet her needs. And these behaviors are **goal-oriented**. The goal of one's behaviors is to meet one's need to belong, to be loved, and to matter. Because these learned behaviors are effective (they work), they may last a lifetime.

The fear of not belonging, not being loved, or not having a purpose is great in people because failing to have one's needs met is to say, "I am rejected; I am not worth loving; and I do not matter to anyone." This is unacceptable to the human psyche since God designed man to function from a place of fullness—man cannot survive with emptiness and deficit (Colossians 2:9–10).

In childhood, these goal-oriented behaviors are fairly simple, but they are strategic. And as the child matures into adulthood, these strategies become more sophisticated. (Review diagram 5 for an overview of these strategies.) Because these goal-oriented behaviors reduce anxiety, they become highly significant to the individual and are fixed in what-the-Bible-calls a *mindset*. Paul says *the mind set on the flesh [strategies to meet my needs] is death, but the mind set on the Spirit [expecting God to meet my needs] is life* (Romans 8:6).

Emotional Responses to Unmet Needs

A person's emotions are a direct result of what he is telling himself about his circumstances. Negative emotions develop when a person tells himself his needs are not being met. And since a man cannot meet his own needs, negative emotions are inevitable: he becomes angry, anxious, or depressed. When one's goal-oriented behaviors are no longer working, what will the person do? He may try to change his behaviors. And in order to do that he may have to change the way he thinks: psychology refers to this as "cognitive restructuring." The Bible provides a higher way: it is called "renewing the mind." But if a person is unwilling to alter his behaviors, thus, changing the way he meets his needs, he will blame others, he will become increasingly anxious, or he will become depressed.

Blocked Goals result in Anger: if a person convinces himself that someone else is responsible for blocking his goals, he will become angry. He determines someone else is preventing him from doing the thing that makes him feel safe. For example, this could happen in marriage when one spouse demands that the other spouse change a certain behavior, or it could happen in a work place when the boss criticizes an employee's work performance.

Note: Let me give an example of this that everyone can identify with. Let us suppose that I come home from work one afternoon early and because I am hungry, I decide to have a can of soup since dinner is still two hours away. In the kitchen, I go to the second drawer where we keep the can-opener. It is not there. I am irritated, saying to my self "someone didn't put the can-opener back in the right drawer." Then I start looking in the third drawer (you know, the one that is messy because everything but the kitchen sink is in that drawer!). It's not there either. I begin to yell out to the living room where my children and wife are cowering and hoping I don't fly into a rage. Gradually, my children slink into their rooms and my wife cowers in the corner. Now, I ask you this question: "What am I angry about?" Your response is probably "you are angry because you can't find the can-opener." NO! That is not really why I am angry. I am REALLY angry because one of my needs is not being met! Which one? My need to matter. My anger, a blocked goal, indicates that I NEED my order, my control over things and my family, in order to feel like I matter. Unknowingly, I am saying to myself "if my family really respected me, if I mattered to them, they would put the can-opener in the right place." I have defined "mattering" as everything being the way I want; I have defined my self as being "effective" when people do what I say, when I am in control. My family is blocking my goal.

Uncertain Goals result in Anxiety: when someone's life is in transition and he is unable to continue earlier goal-oriented behaviors, he will be anxious. Anxiety, remember, is that feeling of fear that my needs will not be met. People always feel anxious when they are going through a major change in their lives because the familiar ways for meeting their needs may no longer be possible. For example, moving to a new state, starting a new job, changing schools, getting married, having a child can be the source of anxiety.

Unreachable Goals result in Depression: when a person tells himself that his behaviors are not effective any longer, that he will never get his needs met, he becomes depressed. For example, this most often happens to a woman when she tells herself she cannot be OK in a marriage since her husband is not meeting her needs. It also happens to a man when he feels he is in a "dead-end" job. It will also happen to a man when he believes he will never able to meet his wife's demands for more than he is able to give her.

Note: Let us use the "can-opener" example, above, to illustrate depression. If I tell my self that my family doesn't respect me and never will, I am set up for depression. I am telling my self that something that "needs to happen" will never happen. I will never get the control over my family that I 'need;' I will never be respected. My goal-oriented behavior is not only blocked; my goal "to matter" is unreachable.

Diagram 9

EMOTIONAL RESPONSES TO UNMET NEEDS

AS A PERSON DEVELOPS...

QUESTIONS NEEDING TO BE ANSWERED ARE:

1. **FROM BIRTH**
   A child's life begins with
   UNMET NEEDS

   - *Do I belong?*
   - *Am I loved?*
   - *Do I matter?*

2. **MENTALLY**
   A child develops a
   belief structure that
   results in
   WRONG THINKING AND BELIEFS

   - *How do I view myself?*
   - *What do I think about myself?*

3. **VOLITIONALLY**
   In order to meet his
   needs, the child
   develops
   GOAL-ORIENTED BEHAVIORS

   - *How do I meet my needs?*

4. **EMOTIONALLY**
As a result of Unmet Needs, the child/adult experiences

PAINFUL EMOTIONS

When Goals are **BLOCKED, ANGER** is the response.

When Goals are **UNCERTAIN, ANXIETY** is the response.

When Goals are **UNREACHABLE, DEPRESSION** results.

THE STORY OF MARTHA ILLUSTRATES THE CORRELATION BETWEEN UNMET NEEDS AND NEGATIVE EMOTIONAL RESPONSES

The New Testament story of Jesus' dinner visit to the home of Mary and Martha (Luke 10) provides an excellent illustration of the correlation between one's beliefs, behaviors, and feelings. Before expositing this passage, let me begin with a personal reflection that will give the reader a deeper appreciation of this occasion when Jesus came to dinner at the home of Martha and Mary.

In January 1977, I boarded a plane at Dulles Airport, Washington D.C., with 40 other Peace Corps volunteers, bound for Kabul, Afghanistan. There I would spend the next two years teaching English as a second language. Though I had been academically trained for the cross-cultural differences I would be facing, I could have in no way been prepared psychologically for this journey back into medieval time. Through the automobile, airplane, electricity and telephone the twentieth century had been introduced to this time-arrested country. Yet the culture and traditions of this isolated mountain region had not really changed since the time of Gangus Khan when barbaric warriors rode horseback over the rugged mountain terrain savagely attacking their enemies and protecting life in this cruel land.

As a high school English teacher in an all-male boarding school in Kabul, I had the unique opportunity of traveling around the various provinces, where I was the recipient of oriental hospitality. In many Afghan homes I was "the" dinner guest and even on occasion, an overnight guest. Daily lifestyle in Afghanistan is peculiarly reminiscent of Old Testament Bible times. Instead of sitting on chairs, and eating at a table—a Western convention—Afghans eat while reclining on pillows on the floor. They eat with their hands, not utensils. Also, they eat out of common bowls, not having individual plates, as we are accustomed. An Afghan woman carries a large vessel on her head as she walks to the community well (reminiscent of John's account of the "woman at the well"). Men and women are separated in social settings. Often, since I would not even meet the hostess of a home where I happened to dine, I would have to pass on my compliments through the male host because the females remained for the entire evening in the kitchen, or in other designated female quarters.

On such a special occasion, the Afghan women would always receive help from their extended family and neighbors with the dinner preparations. In fact, the preparation itself was a major part of the event. There would generally be anywhere from 6 to 12 entrees, all prepared without the aid of the modern conveniences we take for granted. Since a refrigerator was beyond the means of most Afghan households (if they even had electricity), all ingredients had to be purchased the day they were used. One popular food that was almost always served was a pasta dish something like Italian raviolis. Imagine the work to make raviolis from scratch, especially without the aid of a pasta machine or even a rolling pin! Adding to the difficulty, provincial women would have no running water or electricity and would simply be squatting on the floor of a room designated for cooking. If the home had electricity, there would be a hot plate. Without electricity, there would be a small coal-burning stove on the floor.

And in addition to the members of the extended family, it was not unusual for even poor Afghans to have servants. These servants were often children from even poorer Afghan families who were unable to provide the barest necessities of life. So they would indenture their children to a more "prosperous" family.

The story of Mary and Martha has become especially meaningful to me after my return from Afghanistan. Having been a dinner guest in an Afghan home, I can easily understand the cultural setting of the story where Jesus goes to the home of Lazarus where his sisters Mary and Martha are engaged in meal preparations according to the customs of their day. The meal preparation that day for their highly honored guest must have been very similar to that of an Afghan home: the more honored the guest, the greater the number of "dishes" that would be served.

With this personal introduction, the scene is now set for our exposition and interpretation of this Biblical narrative in which Martha's attitudes, behaviors, and feelings are so insightfully displayed.

> Now as they were traveling along, He entered a certain village; and a woman named Martha welcomed him into her home. And she had a sister called Mary, who moreover was listening to the Lord's word, seated at His feet. But Martha was distracted with all her preparations; and she came up to Him, and said, 'Lord do you not care that my sister has left me to do all the serving alone? Then tell her to help me.' But the Lord answered and said to her, 'Martha, Martha, you are worried and bothered about so many things; but only a few things are necessary, really only one, for Mary has chosen the good part, which shall not be taken away from her.'
>
> (Luke 10:38–42)

Martha's words reveal so much about her feelings:

- *Lord, do You not care* [blaming Jesus for not caring about her]
- *that my sister* [the impersonal reference distances her emotionally]
- *has left me* [perceived abandonment; she doesn't belong]
- *to do all* [perceived abuse; under-appreciated]
- *the serving* [this is what makes Martha feel like she matters]
- *alone* [perceived abandonment; she doesn't belong]
- *Then tell her to help me* [Notice that Martha does not wait for Jesus to answer: she has a strong expectation of what Jesus should do.]

Clearly, Martha is both *anxious* and *angry*! John's account reveals the psychological interaction between Jesus and Martha and how Jesus diagnoses Martha's problem.

Jesus Blocks Martha's Goal-oriented Behaviors!

The Americans in Afghanistan who had the most successful cross-cultural experience were those who were willing to let go of their own traditions and expectations to embrace fully those of their Afghan hosts. Imagine if you had an Afghan guest in your home who refused to eat at your table, insisting that you and your family sit on the floor, or who rejected the use of his own plate, eating instead from yours—with his fingers! Turn that around and you have a sense of the indignity that our Afghan hosts must have felt toward an American guest preferring to eat from his own plate, refusing his host's offer of the shared bowl.

Martha was like these ethnocentric Americans, full of expectations about how things are supposed to be. Using Paul's words, Martha had been *conformed to her world* (Romans 12:2). Martha had learned and accepted the contemporary cultural expectations of a woman. Why? Conforming to these cultural expectations was Martha's way of meeting her need to belong, be loved, and to matter. Specifically, her need to belong, to be considered worthy (loved), and to matter were based on how well she performed the task of caring for the home, preparing a meal, and entertaining a guest. As long as she performed well, she could *control* the way people responded to her. Thus she was *in control* of meeting her own needs. Martha's conformity to people's expectations was, at first, learned from outside of her self, but then the expectations became internalized. And once internalized, these behaviors were automatic—a person does not even think about it!

Thus, John's narrative shows Martha's negative emotional responses as she complains to Jesus that Mary (and indirectly Jesus) is not conforming to the conventional rules. Jesus is blocking Martha's goal to matter. Perhaps, feeling alone and even abandoned, Jesus is perceived as blocking her goal to belong. And third, is it possible that the acceptance of Mary's behavior by Jesus causes Martha to feel comparatively less valued for the things she was doing?

In his response to her, Jesus defines Martha's problem [pay close attention to Him!]. He says she is *worried* and *bothered* (*Martha, you are worried and bothered about so many things . . .*). Let us look at these two words.

Worried means Anxious

The word *worry* is also translated *anxious* by Jesus in the Sermon on the Mount (Matthew 6:31) and by Paul in his letter to the Philippians (4:6). This is our natural reaction to danger, poverty, hunger and other troubles that befall us in daily life. Oppressed by the burdens of life, our innate feeling is one of powerlessness. Since we were created to operate in power (Adam was given rule and authority over the earth) our response to losing that control leaves us feeling anxious. This was Adam's initial feeling when he sinned. Martha was full of anxious thoughts such as: "Why is Lazarus allowing Mary to be out with the men?" "Why isn't Jesus telling Mary to help in the kitchen?" "Why am I in here with all the servants?" The real reason Martha was anxious was because she doubted that things she was doing were going to achieve the acknowledgment and rewards she wanted.

Bothered means Angry

The word *bother* means the *outward expression of mental agitation*. In a word, *anger*. When we fail at meeting our needs—and if we believe someone else is responsible for it—we become angry. Adam was the first one to do this—he blamed God for giving him Eve. Martha's angry feelings confirm that she blames Jesus. Jesus is breaking Martha's *rules* by sanctioning Mary's neglect of them. Jesus is blocking Martha's goal-oriented behaviors that are designed to make her feel she matters. Feeling un-affirmed for her choices, Martha cannot feel that she belongs (the men are in separate activity from the women and Martha is not part of them); she cannot feel a sense of worth (her work is devalued); she cannot meet her need to matter by preparing dishes. Many people are like Martha, raging against an out-of-control universe where our needs are not met. Martha's anger is a normal response to this loss of control.

Martha's Behavior Shows How She is Trying to Meet Her Needs

Martha's anxiety and anger reveal her goal-oriented behaviors. If we were to ask the question: "what was Martha angry about?" most people would answer: "Martha was angry about doing all the work by herself." But something below the surface is the real reason for Martha's anger.

Martha believes she needs to behave in a certain way in order to meet her need to belong, to be acceptable, and to matter. Martha's strategy is to be the best homemaker and hostess she can be. And when this works, she feels good about herself. It makes her feels safe; she is in control. Martha had not only defined herself in this way, but she also had determined that this was how other women, including Mary, ought to do to define themselves as well. Like many people, and like my American friends in Afghanistan, Martha assumed her values and beliefs were "right." But she still required the affirmation and validation of those around her.

Martha felt OK about herself, or in control, as long as the rules stayed the same. But when the rules changed, she felt unsafe, nervous, and threatened. Like Martha, we have cultivated our sense of safety around these learned behaviors, *flesh strategies,* that make us feel we are in control. Jesus came into Martha's home, into her comfort zone, and shook things up. Jesus was a threat to the status quo. We must wonder: had anyone ever challenged Martha up to that point? Jesus challenged the assumptions of the traditionalists of his day. Symbolically, Jesus came to shake up the world. He calls believers out of their privately ordered worlds of safety and security and calls them to let go. He wants his followers to exchange their *control* for His, to be God-centered, no longer self-centered.

The story of Martha illustrates our counseling paradigm: she is anxious in the kitchen when her needs are not met; her anxiety turns into anger in the parlor when she blames Mary and Jesus for not validating her; and Martha is headed for depression if her behaviors no longer work, resulting in an unreachable goal.

Jesus Redefines Life for Us, Telling Us What is Really Important

Referring again to Jesus' earlier words to Martha, Jesus cuts through the complexity of culture and tradition when He says, *only one thing is really important.* The problem is that believers are so preoccupied with trying to meet their needs they miss that one "thing." Mary saw it: she chose Jesus. She was occupied with the *one thing.* She was single-minded; Martha was preoccupied with many things: she was double-minded. As a result, she was troubled. I wonder if the "one thing" reminded Mary of David's words in Psalm 27:4 *One thing I have asked from the Lord, that I shall seek: that I may dwell in the house of the Lord all the days of my life.* It is a matter of priority. Paul also confirmed the *one thing* when he said *Brethren, I do not regard myself as having laid hold of it yet; but one thing I do: forgetting what lies behind and reaching forward to what lies ahead* (Philippians 3:13–14). Paul's *one thing* was total occupation with knowing Christ.

He was single-minded. Paul reminds us this is what happened in the Garden: *I am afraid, lest as the serpent deceived Even by his craftiness, your minds should be led astray from the simplicity and purity of devotion to Christ* (2 Corinthians 11:3). As Eve was tempted away from her single-minded focus to be occupied with something else, so today believers can be so occupied with *many things* they miss the *one thing.*

Our counselees are out of focus as they arrive at the counseling office. They are out of sorts because they are so focused on the issues, the problems, their failures, and the failures of others. The most important thing we can do is to help them focus on what is really important. They are preoccupied with their self life; we must help them move forward to be occupied with Christ.

Back to Alice

When Alice understood the relationship between her anger and her "goal" to perform well as a way of proving she was worthy, she was able to let go of that behavior. Alice was more comfortable when she meditated on God's unconditional love of her. She put off the "old way" of thinking about herself and enjoyed the "new self" as she had never understood it before. She began a new walk of freedom. She was free to have an imperfect house and children who made mistakes. As she grew in grace, she was able to extend grace to herself, and more importantly, to her children. The more she let go of the "need" to be in control, the more Alice's anger diminished. The children's bad behavior was no longer a blocked goal because the goal had changed. Instead of expecting others, or her self to "perform," Alice's goal was to find her pleasure in God's unconditional love and acceptance of her. As long as she mattered to God, that was all that mattered to Alice.

CHAPTER TEN

Developing a Treatment Plan

I n this chapter, we will identify the five steps of the counseling process. As you read through the steps, it might be helpful to keep in mind that effective counseling is necessarily brief. To "lay counselors" I recommend that counseling be limited to between six and eight sessions. There are two reasons for this:1) the majority of counselees will not remain in counseling for a long time; and 2) the greatest effectiveness in counseling happens in the initial meetings. As counseling continues, its effectiveness is subject to the law of diminishing returns.

Step One: Engaging

In the first appointment, the counselor's objective is to:

1) Build Rapport
2) Set Boundaries/Limits
3) Identify Reason for Counseling
4) Explore Relevant History

Building rapport through preliminary and initial conversations with the counselee is necessary in establishing a caring, safe environment. As you prepare for your first meeting with this counselee, it will help to think how you would feel if you were in the counselee's position. It is important that your counselee knows you care for him as a brother or sister in Christ. Be positive in letting the counselee know you can help him. Assure the counselee of your competence through your training program. You must communicate with confidence that you do understand the counselee's problem and are able to develop a counseling strategy that will be helpful. Often counselees will ask the counselor questions like: "Have you been trained in 12-step programs?" "Do you have experience counseling sexual addicts?" "Have you ever counseled a pyromaniac?" They are looking for experience because they believe that is the only way for someone to understand and treat their problem. You must not be threatened or intimidated by such questions. Strategic Biblical Counseling does not focus on "issues." But at this point, the counselee would not be able to understand that. You need only respond: "I believe I have been adequately trained to help you with your problem."

Setting boundaries or limits is essential. Let the counselee know how important this time is for you. Let the counselee know your expectations about punctuality, the number and frequency of sessions, what to expect in each counseling session: in this way, if you have problems later on, you can refer back to this first meeting. Also, it is necessary to let the counselee know that you will be assigning homework, in the form of reading and activities, and how crucial the counselee's cooperation is. And finally, assure him of your confidentiality to anything that is shared in the counseling office (with the exception of child abuse, which is a reportable crime).

Begin by asking your counselee why he is seeking help at this time. This will help you focus the counselee. In most cases, the problem(s) for which he has come to see you have been occurring for some time, so ask the question: "what has recently happened that made you seek help for this problem now?" The counselee may have had a conflict with a spouse or a friend. Perhaps it is a behavior that has been out of control for some time, but recently has become increasingly difficult and/or troublesome.

Ask probing questions that will elicit relevant, significant information. If the counselor is not clear about what he wants to know, the counselee may give too much unnecessary and irrelevant historical information. Remember: your counselee will probably come in to a counseling appointment with some preconceived ideas. By asking about the most recent catalyst that led the counselee to seek help, and working backward toward other recent, and therefore relevant, incidents, the counselor will understand the counselee's immediate stress.

Step Two: Diagnosis

In order for any "treatment" to be effective, it must be preceded by an accurate diagnosis. There is an inevitable, logical connection between diagnosis and treatment. If the counselor misdiagnoses the problem, his treatment will miss the mark. If on the other hand, he rightly discerns the root of the problem, the counseling will be successful.

It is crucial that Biblical counselors discern the counselee's underlying problems. Do not get trapped trying to deal with the external issues presented by the counselee. When this happens, the counselee takes leadership; he directs the counseling session. Remember: the counselee will want to talk about the issues; the Biblical counselor wants to find the root cause—to see the heart. Ultimately, the Biblical counselor's objective is to help the counselee see the connection between his "failed" goal-oriented behaviors and his unmet need(s).

There are three elements in diagnosing the problem

The following paradigm makes diagnosing any issue relatively easy. It relies on a simple construct: fear and anxiety cause people to develop strategies early in life to try to meet their needs. (Read chapter 5, *What is Wrong with Me?*).

1. Identify Problem Feelings

(Reference: chapter 9, *Feelings: What Good are They?*)

The first and most obvious thing that will happen as counseling begins (first session), is that the counselee will tell the counselor how he feels. This is almost always the reason that the counselee is seeking help. I say *almost always* because there are some counselees, more often men, who are struggling with addiction or other issues and are aware of a cognitive dissonance, but may not *know* how they are feeling. In such cases, the Biblical counselor should help the counselee identify his "feelings."

Feelings are crucial because they will lead the counselor to discover the counselee's self-destructive thought patterns, beliefs, expectations, and ultimately, his unmet need(s). This provides the basis for the treatment plan.

Note: One time a man came to see me confessing to an addiction to pornography. After explaining his problem to me, I asked "and how do you feel about this?" He responded with ambivalence, saying he didn't know how he felt. I further questioned, "Are you depressed?" "No," he responded, "I am a very optimistic person; I never get depressed." "Are you anxious?" I asked. "No," he said, "I am never anxious." Well then, I probed, "Are you angry or bothered about your behavior?" "Not really," he said, "I just know it is wrong." My next question really surprised him. "If you don't feel bad about your behavior, why do you want to change?" He was shocked that I, a Biblical counselor, was asking him why he wanted to change this obvious sinful behavior. My point, as I explained to him, was that if he was not "feeling" any pain about his behavior, there was little chance he would suffer through the hard choices ahead. Without negative feelings, there would be little motivation. It is certainly a truism that pain causes people to change. As we continued counseling, I assured him that if he stopped using pornography (it had become a daily habit), he would surely start to feel depressed. And of course, he did. Then we were able to identify his unmet needs and develop a treatment plan.

2. Identify Problem Behaviors

(Reference: chapter 8: "Making Better Choices")

Another thing that will happen is the confession of sinful behaviors. Counselees may be embarrassed, however, and therefore somewhat cautious in revealing the scope or depth of the problem behavior. For example, a man struggling with anger may confess he gets angry, but it may be several sessions before he confesses that he gets enraged and knocks his fist through the wall. Also, people often understate sexual misconduct because of shame. An effective counselor will ask probing questions to explore the scope of the problem.

Note: I counseled a man who was dealing with anger and depression. I had no idea he was having such terrible rages until his wife came in to see me one day and explained how her husband frequently threw things at her: a coffee mug, a book. She said he had broken the TV once by throwing things at the screen.

Other problem behaviors are less evident. For example, a man may have a habit of withdrawing from his wife and children when he is feeling overwhelmed by stress. He may justify the behavior, not seeing it as wrong, nor seeing it as a fleshly strategy to avoid feeling inadequate.

Behaviors are learned over time. They are the choices/actions we have learned in response to feeling anxious (a result of unmet needs). Behaviors are goal-oriented, that is, the goal of any behavior is ultimately to meet a need. One's behaviors are the ways he has learned to deal with the stress of living in a fallen world—a broken home, a failed relationship, and various forms of rejection and abuse.

The Biblical counselor knows that behaviors are an outward display of what is going on in the heart of a person. Jesus said it is not what goes into a man that defiles him, but what comes out of him (out of his heart). (Review chapter 8 to see the correlation between choices and character.) By looking at a counselee's behaviors (his choices) the counselor can learn much about the counselee's self image and self esteem.

It is very important to look for the less evident behaviors to determine the direction of counseling. In order to be successful, the counselor and counselee will need to be specific in addressing what needs to be *put off* so the counselee can be *renewed in his thinking*, and thus *put on the Lord Jesus Christ.*

3. Identify Problem Thinking

(Reference: chapter 6: *Can I Change?* and chapter 8, *Making Better Choices*)

In the third step of diagnosis, the counselor begins to evaluate the counselee's belief system—his self-destructive thought patterns. Paul tells the Corinthians to *take every thought captive to the obedience of Christ* (2 Corinthians 10:5). Every thought and every belief one holds on to must be examined in light of what God says. The Word of God is the counselor's reference point and his plumb line.

Identifying the counselee's wrong thinking helps the counselor to hone in on values and beliefs he must "put off" along with his wrong behaviors. As the counselor listens to the counselee, discerns underlying beliefs, and listens to the Holy Spirit, he begins to form a strategy for his counseling sessions of what truths need to be taught—and revealed by the Holy Spirit—if the counseling is to be successful.

For more on problem thinking, please refer to chapter 8, *Making Better Choices*, "Real Knowledge."

Diagram 10

Step Two: Diagnosis

HOW DOES THE COUNSELOR IDENTIFY UNMET NEEDS AND WRONG GOALS?		
Step One From the "Engaging" Phase, the counselor should be able now to answer the following questions: • *Is the counselee most deficient in belonging?* • *Is the counselee most deficient in love/acceptance?* • *Is the counselee most deficient in feeling effective?*		Problem FEELINGS are the product of problem BEHAVIORS that reveal what the counselee BELIEVES he must do to meet his needs. This "feeling-behaving-believing" complex is what Paul calls the "mindset of the flesh" (Roman 8:5). The objective of this step is to begin to discern deficits.

Step
 	
Two
 	
Identify Problem Feelings
	ANGER IS A BLOCKED GOAL:
	  If counselee is angry, it is because he is blaming someone else for not meeting his need.
	ANXIETY IS AN UNCERTAIN GOAL:
	  Anxiety is the consequent feeling when counselee is going through changes (his needs used to be met in a certain way but changes require new, untested ways).
	DEPRESSION IS AN UNREACHABLE GOAL:
	  Counselee has given up hope of ever getting his needs met.	

Step **Three** Identify Problem Behaviors	*How does counselee meet his needs?*	Problem behaviors identify STRATEGIES the counselee has employed to meet his needs. STRATEGIES are directly related to GOALS. GOALS are what the counselee tells himself must happen in order for his needs to be met, e.g. "I must get people to like me" or "I must succeed in sports to be accepted." (See Chapter 5, "What is Wrong with Me?")
Step **Four** Identify Problem Thinking	*How does counselee view himself?* *What does counselee think of himself?*	Problem thinking reveals the "beliefs" that underlie the GOALS the counselee has unconsciously set in place in order to meet his need to belong, to be loved and accepted, and to matter.

Diagram 11

Example of Diagnosis

EXAMPLE: SALLY, a 38 year old married woman **How does the counselor identify Sally's unmet needs and wrong goals?**	
Step One **Is the counselee most deficient in:** *belonging?* *love/acceptance?* *feeling effective?*	Sally feels like she cannot keep up with the demands of her life. She has two children in grade school. Her husband returns from work too tired to talk with her. He doesn't ask her about her day. He doesn't affirm her for what she does to keep the house clean or take care of the children. In fact, he is critical. She doesn't "feel" appreciated.
Step Two Identify Problem Feelings	Sometimes Sally feels angry and other times she is depressed. The reason she seeks counseling is that she is angry with her husband and has become increasingly impatient with the children. Her anger is spiraling out of control.
Step Three Identify Problem Behaviors	Sally fights and conflicts with her husband daily; he says she is nagging him. Sally yells at the children and calls them "stupid" and/or "idiots" if they make a mistake. Feeling guilty, she tries harder to keep the house clean and "be there" for the kids' activities.
Step Four Identify Problem Thinking	Sally has been telling herself for years that the only way to be acceptable and feel appreciated is to perform well. She has always been able to excel in whatever she has done. Maybe she should never have married and had children.

Conclusion: Sally's anger is a blocked goal. Her goal to be "effective," even perfect, is blocked by 1) a husband who doesn't validate but criticizes her and 2) children who don't "do what they are supposed to" (this makes her look like a bad parent). She has never learned how to draw upon her relationship with Christ to "feel" effective. When she feels inadequate, God seems distant to her.
Now the counselor is ready to set goals, facilitate right thinking, and help change behaviors.

Step Three: Setting Goals

After the problem has been identified, you and your counselee will determine what goals they can reasonably accomplish in the limited amount of sessions they will have together. There is a common saying: "those who fail to plan, plan to fail." An effective counselor knows the importance of setting goals.

> *Note: A man scheduled an appointment with me because he wanted a "second opinion." He had been seeing a therapist for four years and had recently asked his therapist how close he thought they were to being finished. The therapist had answered the man: "we're about half-way there." When the counselee told me this, I remember thinking to myself: "half-way where?" Clearly, this counselee was not aware of his counselor's goals. And worse, the counselee had no clear understanding of his own objectives for counseling. There was no mutually agreed upon objective for what the counselor and counselee were attempting to accomplish.*

Setting goals with a counselee at the onset of counseling does four things.

    a. It **prevents passivity**. The counselor is letting his counselee know that he expects him to take responsibility for and engage in the treatment plan. He must "own" it.

    b. It **establishes the direction** of the counseling, and keeps the treatment plan on track.

        It is not unusual for counselees to have lives that are generally out of order. One week, the counselee will present one issue as his problem, and three weeks later, something else. It is crucial for successful counseling not to allow the counselee's disorder to determine the direction of the counseling session.

    c. It strengthens **accountability**.

    d. It is a way to **measure progress**.

Goals must be Realistic, Measurable, and Flexible

Realistic

Goals that are not realistic will result in aborted counseling when the counselee becomes discouraged. Let's suppose that a counselee "Joan" is having problems dealing with her anger toward her husband and children. She tells you she wants to "get over" her anger "once and for all." This is not realistic, and Joan will undoubtedly leave counseling believing she has failed or that you failed in helping her with her problem! A proper goal might be to understand why she gets angry, or to learn to deal appropriately with her feelings, or to practice self control (see chapter 11, *A Strategic Treatment Plan for Anger*).

Measurable

Goals that are not measurable will result in frustration and eventual despair when the counselee does not see any change. If Joan seeks counseling because she is angry, the goal of "learning to deal appropriately with her feelings" must be broken into measurable components: fewer angry outbursts or fewer sarcastic responses are things (actions) that are measurable. She will come in to her appointments eager to tell you about little successes. It is very important for the counselor to affirm progress and keep the counselee focused on the process, not the final product.

Flexible

Goals need to be flexible so they can be changed if necessary in the course of counseling. For example, if Joan is having trouble in her marriage, her first goal might be to be less destructive with her anger. However, after a few appointments, the emphasis in counseling shifts from her anger at her husband to her dissatisfaction and disappointment with God. Then her goal may be changed to "how can I develop more intimacy with the Lord?" You may ask, "is it OK to change the goal?" It is very OK when it means the counselee has gotten in touch with a deeper heart issue.

Counselees do not always find it easy to articulate their goals or objectives in counseling. But if the counselee is not engaged in making these decisions, he will be more inclined to sit back and let the counselor do all the work.

Consider using one of these questions to help the counselee in setting his goals

1. What do you want to see different as a result of counseling?
2. When we have finished, what would make you say that this was worth your time?
3. What would need to happen so that you no longer need counseling?

Step Four: Apply Truth to Wrong Thinking

The fourth step in counseling is the critical stage: the Biblical counselor communicates truth to the counselee. Unfortunately, this is where many well-intentioned lay counselors fail. Rather than discern what the counselee's faulty thinking is, and apply appropriate truth, they commit one of two mistakes. 1) They give pat answers (one size fits all!): *just trust God; have faith; God is in control; God still loves you; God is good,* etc. 2) They give advice—not Biblical counsel—that emanates from their own experience: *when I was your age . . . ; when I was experiencing what you are going through, I . . .* , etc.

In both cases, counselors may not be listening to the Holy Spirit to discern the real heart issue. In the first case, the counselor is using Scripture in a "mental" way. There is no power in mental counseling since spiritual truth can only be communicated by the Holy Spirit and *in spirit*. The Spirit-led counselor takes the *logos* and waits for the Holy Spirit to communicate a specific word to the counselee—a *rhema, like apples of gold in settings of silver is a word spoken in right circumstances* (Proverbs 25:11). Second, in the advice-giving approach, the counselor's reference point is himself—not the Word of God. This is a common mistake made by many well-intentioned mature Christians. There is a place for advice, but it must be distinguished from Biblical counseling.

Knowing what truth to apply to wrong thinking requires the counselor to pray and listen to the Holy Spirit. Paul prays for the Philippians (1:9–10) that they will grow in discernment so that they will excel in making better decisions. Biblical counselors must take a different path, a higher strategy. This can only happen as the Biblical counselor operates in true spiritual discernment (See chapter 8, *Making Better Choices, Discernment.*)

What is the "Truth" that Biblical Counselors Apply to Wrong Thinking?

The Biblical counselor should assure that his counselee understands his identity in Christ. I have never had a counselee who had a perfect understanding of his new nature. Most, if not all, counselees approach counseling focused on the "old self," unaware of the truth that the "old self was crucified with Christ."

Many counselees do not understand God's process of sanctification. They are almost always unable to see how the trial they are going through is connected to God's bigger picture. Biblical counselors provide new eyes for seeing circumstances. Even in secular therapy, this practice is commonly understood. A common construct of psychologists is to **re-frame** the counselee's issues. Who better to re-frame an issue than a counselor who can provide a Biblical perspective?

Following is a summary of essential truth that the Biblical counselor will communicate to every counselee.

1) Truth about one's sinful patterns of thinking and behavior: most counselees are not conscious of their self-defeating beliefs. (Reference Chapter 5 and 7) *And put off the old self which is being corrupted in accordance with the lusts of deceit* (Eph 4:2).
2) Truth about one's identity in Christ: most counselees are still defining themselves as the "sons of Adam" rather than the "sons of God." (Reference Chapters 3 and 6) *As many as received Him [Christ] to them gave He [God] the authority to become the children [sons] of God* (John 1:12).
3) Truth about the power to change because of the counselee's union with Christ. (Reference Chapter 6) *Knowing this, that the old self was crucified with Christ . . . that we should no longer be slaves to sin* (Romans 6:6).
4) Truth about the process of change: many counselees do not understand the process of walking in the Spirit. (Reference chapter 7) *If you walk by the Spirit you will no longer carry out the desire of the flesh . . . if you are putting to death the deeds of the body, you will live* (Galatians 5:16; Romans 8:13).

How Does The Counselee Replace Wrong Thinking With Right Thinking?

This step requires the counselee's cooperation. Teaching and re-framing will not affect the counselee's thought life unless he commits to *see* through the Biblical lens.

First, the mind must be *renewed* (Romans 12:2).

Though the human spirit is made alive when the believer becomes a child of God, it is only through the renewing of the mind that the soul is transformed. The renewing of the mind means filling the mind with truth, meditating upon it until it begins to change the person from the very core of his being—inside-out.

Second, the mind must be *controlled* (2 Corinthians 10:5).

In order to attain and hold on to a right mindset, believers must learn to control their thoughts. In 1 Peter 1:13 the command is given to *gird up the loins of your mind, and be sober.* Just as a Roman soldier would tuck up his skirt under his belt before running into a battle, a person is to gather up the loose ends of his thinking. Instead of allowing his thoughts to run hither and yon, he is to gather them in and keep them under his control. Paul says *take every thought captive to the obedience of Christ.* Unless the mind is controlled, the believer will experience much hindrance to his spiritual maturity, and will have little peace of mind.

Third, the mind must be *occupied* (Philippians 4:8).

The mind must be occupied with thoughts that are positive and profitable. The believer is to direct his thoughts with purpose and meaning. This means the mind must be actively engaged all the time. A blank mind produces a passive will. The mind must be occupied with noble thoughts. Paul says: *Whatever is true, whatever is honorable, whatever is right, whatever is pure, whatever is lovely, whatever is of good repute, if there is any excellence and if anything worthy of praise, let your mind dwell on these things.*

ASSIGNING HOMEWORK

One of the primary ways to help the counselee effect these changes in his thinking is to provide homework reading assignments. This can be by way of recommended books, magazine articles, and of course, Scriptural passages for meditating and memorizing. Every Biblical counselor should have a file of reading materials that he will use appropriately. Like a doctor prescribing medicine, the Biblical counselor prescribes Scripture reading, study, memorization, and meditation.

Step Five: Secure Commitment to Biblical Behavior

As stated in chapter 8, *Making Better Choices,* every counselee will almost certainly have some behavior that is sabotaging his spiritual and emotional progress. Therefore, the counselee must commit himself to make changes in his behavior to be consistent with a new mindset. If he does not, his personal progress will be impeded and the counseling process unnecessarily extended.

These changes can be summarized in two Biblical principles:

First, **repentance** is essential to salvation, and is a foundational block of sanctification. It is necessary that the counselee exercise true repentance in order to expect God's life-changing power. Repentance means a turning from the "old" pursuits and turning to a new way of looking at things. The door is open for renewing the mind, healing the emotions, and aligning the will. Scripture asserts that repentance produces radical change in all three areas: the mind (Matthew 3:2, Mark1:15), the heart (Matthew 21:29, 32; Hebrews 7:21), and the will (Matthew 3:8; 9:13; Acts 20:21). Repentance moves a person to take a violent stand against his wrong behavior and paves the way to radical departure from sin. Failure to lead the counselee into repentance will not only result in ineffective counseling, but will contribute to *easy-believism* and *cheap grace*.

Second, **obedience** is the result of the life of true faith. The victorious Christian lives in total dependence on Christ to defeat sin. He even depends on the Holy Spirit to motivate him toward obedience in the heart. Jesus said, *If you love Me, you will keep My commandments*. Saul's disobedience led to the removal of God's blessing on his kingdom. Even a cursory review of Old Testament history reveals that the Israelites continually forgot that obedience to the Lord was the condition for remaining in the land. Fulfillment of the promises under the Mosaic Covenant was conditioned upon Israel's obedience. Even so, many believers do not recognize that their partial obedience results in spiritual impotence. It is essential for the Biblical counselor to stress obedience.

OBEDIENCE MEANS TO *Heed* OR *Pay Attention* TO SO . . . WHAT ARE YOU PAYING ATTENTION TO?

One final word about obedience: the most commonly used word for obedience in the New Testament is the Greek word *hupokuo*. The word *akuo* simply means *to hear.* The compound word means to *pay attention to*. Therefore, obedience means to listen, hear, and pay attention to God. Counselees are used to following their fleshly feelings—in essence, they have been *paying attention to* their sinful desires. Therefore, Biblical counseling is fundamentally redirecting the counselee's attention away from the fleshly desires to Godly desires. Obedience means paying attention to the Word of God and to the promptings of the Spirit.

> *Therefore do not let sin reign in your mortal body that you should obey* [pay attention to] *its lusts.*
>
> (Romans 6:12)

THE DESIRED RESULT: FRUIT OF THE SPIRIT

At some point, there is an expectation that a changed mind will result in new behaviors and changed feelings. Every mature believer knows that feelings do change. At first, the feelings will change in their intensity. Eventually the feelings dissipate. Fleshly feelings of anger, jealousy, strife, etc. will be replaced with love, joy, peace, goodness, etc. A good conscience and a confidence in God's grace become stronger and stronger.

> The writer of Hebrews captures it well when he says: *All discipline [including counseling] for the moment seems not to be joyful but sorrowful. Yet to those who have been trained by it, afterward it yields the peaceful fruit of righteousness* .
>
> (Hebrew 12:11)

However, I must make this cautionary statement about feelings. The goal of effective Biblical counseling is **not** for the counselee to feel better. Mature believers know that feelings are not to be our drivers. Neither are they to be discounted as irrelevant (see chapter 9, *Feelings: What Good are They?*). However, mature believers know that God's process of sanctification emerges through pain and perseverance (Romans 5:3–5). But there is a joy and peace available to believers by God's grace that surpasses all negative feelings.

QUESTIONS:

Why is it important to set boundaries?

What are the three steps in diagnosis?

What are the four reasons for setting goals?

What are some questions that may help the counselee to determine what his goals are?

What are the essential truths that the Biblical counselor will communicate to every counselee?

In what ways (two) is a commitment to Biblical behavior manifested?

Why is homework important?

COUNSELING SESSION INTERVIEW GUIDE

Establishing the Agenda

To be successful, each counseling session requires management and direction to be effective. The counselor should have a Spirit-led strategy. Accordingly, the counselor should have an agenda for each session, but be willing to drop his agenda at any point where the Holy Spirit is leading otherwise. Each session should begin with a prayer that acknowledges the Holy Spirit's agenda and direction.

Take Leadership

The "Ethical Principles and Code of Conduct" for secular psychologists stresses a client's right to self-determination. In other words, psychologists do not take leadership in the same way as a Biblical counselor. As a Spirit-led person, the counselor takes leadership in setting boundaries, determining the direction of the counseling, setting goals, and assigning homework. This is not to say that counselees are not involved in such decisions. (See chapter 10, *Setting Goals*.)

Be Supportive

Let the counselee know that you are interested, that you care and want to understand. Encouragement, of course, comes from visual as well as oral feedback from the counselor. Verbal encouragement is achieved simply by making statements such as "I see" . . . "uh-huh" . . . "is that so?" . . . "Yes, I understand, go on" . . . Brief, interjectory statements such as these tend to encourage the speaker to say more. They indicate that the counselor is attentive and is attaching proper importance to what the counselee is saying.

Do not be Afraid of Silence

The counselor may talk too much because he feels uncomfortable when silence prevails. However, pauses need not be embarrassing or awkward. Silence often draws people out. Pauses are also valuable after a counselee has responded too briefly to a question. Such a pause is often sufficient to convey the impression that the answer needs to be amplified. If silence continues too long, rephrase the question.

Reflective Listening

An essential feature of effective counseling is the art of listening. Effective listening requires considerable practice and involves learning new skills. The counselor is actively receiving the counselee's response while at the same time coordinating it with information already received, and framing a follow-up question. In addition to listening and absorbing the response, listening involves an evaluation of the response — seeking to establish its meaning in relation to earlier comments. This is called reflective listening. Repeating, rephrasing, and reflecting the counselee's feelings is important for the counselee to know he is understood. Reflective listening that is most effective is accomplished by restating the counselee's comments in a way that adds value and significance to what the counselee has said and may even help clarify for the counselee what he is really feeling or believing.

Non-Verbal Communication

A counterpart of and supplement to verbal communication is non-verbal communication. This involves observations by both the counselor and counselee about one another during the course of the counseling session and relates to such things as manner of dress, facial expressions, head-nodding, body posture, hand gestures, eye movements, the seating arrangements, etc. Non-verbal communication is significant in that it supplements the verbal expression of the counselor. It amplifies, underlines, and at times, contradicts what is conveyed verbally. With this caution in mind, the counselor should be aware of her/his own thoughts and feelings and body expressions lest the non-verbal signs inadvertently convey false impressions to the counselee.

Note Taking

Beginning counselors are frequently concerned about taking notes during the session. Taking notes can be a problem if it interferes with the flow of communication distracting the counselor from what the counselee is saying or even distracting the counselee. However, the purpose of the counseling session is gathering facts, and this provides a natural basis for note taking. The counselee does not expect his counselor to be able to retain the information. In fact, the counselee might have more confidence when he sees the counselor writing down information. The counselor who does not write down such information might make the counselee wonder about her/his sincerity and why she/he asked for the information in the first place. Conversely, the counselee may also begin to wonder just what it is that the counselor is writing down. Therefore, the counselor may need to explain the need for note taking. The counselor would explain that this is a way to ensure retention of accurate information.

The general rule for note taking is this: Do not become preoccupied to the degree that continuous writing becomes distracting. Do not let note taking interfere with your attention to what the counselee is saying.

Closing the Session

It is helpful to leave the counselee with a feeling of closure after each session. It is also important there are no unresolved concerns about what was said in the session before the counselee leaves. Therefore, the counselor must end the session with enough time to ask if there are any concerns and give homework or discuss the agenda for the next session. If this is not done, counselees may speculate about concerns. Prayer is the appropriate way to close a counseling session.

Examples of Questions the Counselor Might Ask During Counseling

Salvation:

1. When were you born again? Or how long have you been born again?

Christian Growth

1. How would you describe your Christian walk at this point?
2. What are you presently doing in your devotional life? How would you describe your relationship with the Lord?

Overview of the Problem and solution (some probing questions)

1. What is the problem?
2. What have you done about it?
3. Could you put into one or two sentences what the issue is?
4. When is the last time you had a physical exam?
5. Have you had counseling before?
6. How long? Was it helpful? What did you learn about the problem or yourself?
7. Have you considered the effort and endurance, e.g., the personal cost it will require for you to make these changes?

Avoiding pitfalls

1. Ask open-ended questions.

2. Never make comments that can be construed as passing judgment on the counselee.
3. Avoid long, elaborate or irrelevant explanations by the counselee by tactfully interrupting and re-phrasing the question to re-focus the discussion.

How to Use the Strategic Biblical Counseling Treatment Plan

The goal of the Biblical counselor is to help the counselee start a new walk and return the counselee to "mainstream" care in the church. Strategic Biblical counseling requires a plan. To be effective a strategic treatment plan must be specific. It must address the counselee's needs, set measurable goals, and provide appropriate teaching.

The process of developing a Strategic Treatment Plan involves a logical series of steps that build on each other, much like constructing a house. This is an inappropriate metaphor, considering that our lives are called the "house of God." And each member of the body of Christ is called a "living stone," the sum total of which is the temple of God. We are told to "build up" one another. The Treatment Plan offers each counselor a tool to focus the counseling process and produce measurable results in less time. The Strategic Treatment Plan is to be used in the following fashion:

1. Read and study the relevant Scriptures; choose one or two you will present to your counselee.
2. Review and select a single long-term goal with your counselee.
3. Review short-term goals and select the one(s) you and your counselee agree to be reasonable.
4. Choose relevant interventions/teachings to assist in changing behaviors and replacing wrong thinking with right thinking.
5. Assign homework that supports the process of renewing the mind.

A Strategic Treatment Plan for Anger

PERTINENT SCRIPTURES

James 1:19–20: Let everyone be quick to hear, slow to speak and slow to anger: for the anger of man does not achieve the righteousness of God.

James 4:1 What is the source of quarrels and conflicts among you? Is not the source your pleasures that wage war in your members? You lust and do not have, so you commit murder. And you are envious and cannot obtain; so you fight and quarrel.

Ephesians 4:26–27, 31–32: Be angry and yet do not sin; do not let the sun go down on your anger, and do not give the devil an opportunity . . . Let all bitterness and wrath [wild rage] and anger and clamor [violent outbursts] and slander be put away from you, along with all malice. And be kind to one another, tenderhearted, forgiving each other, just as God in Christ also has forgiven you.

1 Peter 3:8–9: let all be harmonious, sympathetic, brotherly, kind-hearted, and humble in spirit; not returning evil for evil, or insult for insult, but giving a blessing instead; for you were called for that very purpose that you might inherit a blessing.

James 5:8–9: be patient; strengthen your hearts . . . do not complain against one another, that you yourselves may not be judged.

SETTING LONG-TERM GOALS

1. I will be able to recognize and appropriately express my angry feelings as they occur without outbursts or rages. I will be able to practice self-control as a fruit of the Spirit.
2. I will learn to *walk by the Spirit.* I will experience the reality of *crucifying the flesh with its passions and desires* and will manifest the *fruit of the Spirit.*

SETTING SHORT-TERM GOALS

1. I will increase my awareness of the destructive patterns of my communication.
2. I will increase my awareness of the negative impact of my anger.
3. I will decrease the frequency and duration of my angry outbursts.
4. I will become more sensitive to cynicism, sarcasm and other negative attitudes.
5. I will develop specific, spiritually acceptable ways of communicating angry feelings.
6. I will identify my *blocked goals* or *unmet expectations* at the root of my anger.
7. I will verbalize my feelings of anger in a controlled, assertive way (I will be slow to speak and quick to listen).
8. I will learn to practice forgiveness and acceptance of others and of circumstances over which I have no control.

REPLACING WRONG THINKING WITH BIBLICAL THINKING

1. Teach your counselee what it means to be *created in God's image* and to understand his new nature as a spiritual person. Use diagrams 1 and 2.
2. Teach your counselee about God's power to change through our death and resurrection with Christ. Use diagrams 5 and 6.
3. Confront your counselee's angry behaviors and encourage self-control.

   a. Teach your counselee from James 1:19 to slow down and think about what is going on in the moment, in the dynamic between him and the other person, and in his own thoughts and feelings.
   b. Teach your counselee from James 1:20 to realize he will not achieve his objectives through anger. Lead him to repentance.

4. Empathize and assist your counselee to clarify his feelings of hurt and anger by identifying past disappointments and self-defensive patterns.

   a. Look at Adam's response to God and Eve as a defense mechanism, i.e., fear of loss of control, followed by anger, blame, and distancing (Gen 3).
   b. Teach about blocked goals, citing Jesus' words about Martha, using the account of Mary and Martha (Luke 10:38–42).
   c. Use *Emotional Responses to Unmet Needs* to teach Anger as a *blocked goal*.
   d. Identify your counselee's expectations and goals.
   e. Identify counselee's goal-oriented behaviors.

5. Teach your counselee about flesh strategies, using *Strategies to Meet Unmet Needs* (diagram 3).
6. Make sure your counselee understands the struggle involved in making changes, and what it means to *crucify the flesh* (diagrams 7 and 8).
7. Work with your counselee to understand process of forgiveness and acceptance.

HOMEWORK

1. Give your counselee a copy of *Who Am I?* and *Why did God Make Me?* to reflect on the truth of his identity as a *spiritual* person.
2. Give the counselee a copy of *Emotional Responses to Unmet Needs* and ask him to identify his *blocked goals*.
3. Assign counselee to read *Feelings, What Good are They?* to help identify the nature of anger as a blocked goal.
4. Give the counselee a copy of *Strategies to Meet Unmet Needs* (diagram 3) and ask him to identify his own flesh strategies.
5. Give your counselee articles on forgiveness.
6. Assign client to reflect, study and memorize pertinent Scriptures.

Example of a Strategic Treatment Plan for Anger

Case Scenario: Stan

1. Engaging

Build Rapport; Set Boundaries; Identify Reason for Counseling

At his first appointment, Stan told me he had just had a conflict with his stepson Rob. He also told me that this was the main source of conflict between him and his wife. I asked him to tell me about the recent events that led to the conflict with his son and the immediate reason for seeking counsel. Stan had an argument with his stepson the other night and "got in his face." Rob had used his tools and failed to put them back where they belonged. Stan said that he and Rob seemed to be in a constant "power struggle" ever since Rob had became a teenager. Stan admitted that the main reason he came for counseling is that his wife told him if the relationship between him and Rob did not get better, she would leave him. I empathized with him and assured him that I understood such "power struggles" and that through counseling we would gain insight into the problem and be able to develop a plan to deal with his anger.

Relevant History

Stan was 49 years old and had been married to Rita for 7 years; he and his wife had an ongoing conflict over the years when it came to her son Rob (from a previous marriage) who is now 15. This conflict took place, like many before, when he corrected his stepson because he did not put away the tools after using them (some were missing). Stan complained about how Rob is irresponsible, watches too much TV and video games. Stan was resentful that Rob's grandmother spent too much money on clothes and "toys" for him. In Stan's estimation, the problem was that Rob was irresponsible and didn't respect him. And a big part of the problem was that Rob's mother Rita and his grandmother spoiled him by giving him whatever he wanted.

Stan was a college professor; he was very articulate, analytical, and administrative. (It was apparent that Stan likes to be in control.) He came to his appointment with note paper and recent books he had read about teenagers to show me that he really understood teens but didn't know how to get through to Rob. In the course of talking with Stan, I found out that his own father was very emotionally abusive and controlling. I explored this further and learned that he always felt "put down" by his parents. Stan admitted to being impatient, even with his peers. He also related to me that he often felt resentful of his best friend, a man who was unmarried and had few responsibilities.

It was obvious to me that Stan loved the Lord and had a lot of Bible knowledge. He was born again while in college; he was a Bible teacher at his church. He was strongly motivated to improve the relationship with Rob. But he was also concerned about the conflicts between him and his wife; they each had strong differing opinions about how to set boundaries and discipline Rob.

2. Diagnosis (see page 171)

	Diagnosis for Stan
Step One **Is Stan feeling most deficient in:** *Belonging?* *Love and Acceptance?* *Feeling that he matters?*	Stan's stepson Rob is irresponsible and doesn't respect him. His wife and mother-in-law do not agree with Stan's boundaries (cleaning his room, doing chores, etc.) and discipline of Rob. It was apparent that Stan grew up feeling he had to perform well to please his parents. It was not difficult to see that Stan had exaggerated need to be loved and affirmed, to perform well in whatever he did. The disrespect he feels from his family makes him feel that he doesn't matter to them.
Step Two Identify Problem Feelings	Stan is angry. His anger is out of control (he almost hit his son in a recent incident). He is also angry at his wife and his mother-in-law.
Step Three Identify Problem Behaviors	Stan conflicts with his wife almost daily. He says she doesn't respect him. Stan gets enraged and yells at Rob. He is spending more time at work; he doesn't like to come home.
Step Four Identify Problem Thinking	Stan has been telling himself for years that the only way to feel safe is to keep things under control. If his wife and son really respected him they would agree with his boundaries and discipline.

Conclusion: Stan's anger is a blocked goal. His goal to be "in control" and "efficient" is blocked by 1) a wife who doesn't validate but criticizes him and 2) a son who doesn't "do what he is supposed to" (this makes him feel inadequate and he doesn't like that). When he feels inadequate, he distances himself from people. At those times, he doesn't feel close to God. Though Stan knows God loves him unconditionally, he can not help feeling that God must be displeased with him.

3. Setting Goals

Stan and I agreed to the following goals:

1) Stan would pray, practice *slow to speak; quick to listen* in order to reduce the frequency of angry outbursts.
2) Stan and I agreed to work to identify *blocked goals* at the root of his anger.
3) Stan and his wife would come to counseling to work on conflict resolution skills.

4. Replacing Wrong Thinking with Biblical Thinking

1) I taught Stan from James 1:19–20 that God's method of dealing with conflicts was to slow down and think about what is going on at the moment—to become aware of his own blocked goals and to be sensitive to the blocked goals of his son and wife.
2) Stan realized that his "goal" to be in control and to be respected was being blocked by his son's "failure to do what Stan asked" and by his wife's perceived disrespect. As he understood his self-protective strategies, Stan learned that he had to 1) repent of trying to meet his needs through "control" and "performance" (put off the old self) and 2) learn to let Christ meet that need (put on the Lord Jesus Christ).
3) Stan and I were able to clarify the feelings of hurt and anger that resulted from his parents' expectations and work on forgiveness (letting go) of past disappointments.
4) I helped Stan to see that he was still expressing his "old self" and distinguished between himself as a son of Adam and son of God through John 1:12.
5) Stan and I studied Adam's response (his strategies to meet his needs apart from God) i.e., fear of loss of control, followed by anger, blame, and distancing (Gen 3). Using *Emotional Re-*

sponses to Unmet Needs he understood clearly that his anger was a *blocked goal.*

6) I made sure Stan understood the process of *crucifying the flesh,* and what it would take him to change these behaviors (from Galatians 5:16–25, using diagrams 7 and 8).

HOMEWORK

1) I gave Stan a copy of *Who Am I?* and *Why did God Make Me?* to reflect on the truth of his identity as a spiritual person.

2) I assigned Stan to read *Feelings, What Good are They?* to help him understand anger as a blocked goal.

3) I gave Stan a copy of *Strategies to Meet Unmet Needs* (Diagram 3) and asked him to identify his own flesh strategies.

4) I gave Stan a copy of *Emotional Responses to Unmet Needs* and ask him to identify his blocked goals.

5) I assigned Stan to read articles on forgiveness in order to begin working on letting go of unmet expectations and goal-oriented behaviors and move toward forgiveness.

6) I assigned Stan to memorize and reflect on James 1:19–20 and James 4:1.

A Strategic Treatment Plan for Depression

Pertinent Scripture

Psalm 42: 5–6a

Why are you downcast, O my soul?
Why so disturbed within me?
Put your hope in God, for I will yet praise Him, my Savior and my
God.
My soul is downcast within me; therefore, I will remember you.

Psalm 77:2–3, 10

I found myself in trouble and went looking for my Lord;
My life was an open wound that wouldn't heal.
When friends said, "Everything will turn out all right," I didn't
believe a word they said.
I remember God — and shake my head.
I bow my head — then wring my hands.
I'm awake all night — not a wink of sleep.
I can't even say what's bothering me.
I go over the days one by one;

I ponder the years gone by.
I strum my lute all through the night, wondering how to get my
life together.

Once again I'll go over what God has done,
lay out on the table the ancient wonders;
I'll ponder all the things You've accomplished,
and give a long, loving look at Your acts.

[From "The Message" translation, by Eugene Peterson]

Romans 15:13

May the God of all hope fill you with all joy and peace as you trust
in Him, so that you may overflow with hope by the power of the
Holy Spirit.

SETTING LONG-TERM GOALS

1. I will *walk by the Spirit*, maintaining feelings of joy, peace,
   and contentment and be thankful in all things.
2. I will regain a sense of purpose and find God's fulfillment in
   doing the things He created me to do.
3. I will grieve the "loss" (of something or someone) in order to
   reach a place of true acceptance of God's sovereignty and goodness.

SETTING SHORT-TERM GOALS

1. I will identify the source of my depressed feelings.
2. I will identify my negative self-talk and my "lies" and "mis-
   beliefs."
3. I will identify my "feelings of inadequacy" or "unreachable
   goals" at the root of my depression.

4. I will see what God wants to change in me so that I can move beyond depression.
5. I will engage in physical, recreational, and social activities that reflect increased energy and interest.
6. I will forgive and accept others and circumstances in context of God's sovereignty.

REPLACING WRONG THINKING WITH BIBLICAL THINKING

1. Teach your counselee what it means to be *created in God's image* and to understand his new nature as a spiritual person. (Use diagrams 1 and 2.) *P 52 & 58*
2. Teach your counselee about God's power to change through our death and resurrection with Christ. (Use diagrams 5 and 6.)
3. Use *Emotional Responses to Unmet Needs* to teach depression as an *unreachable goal.*
4. Help your counselee to see his negative self-talk and commit to replace it with right thinking (Philippians 4:8).
5. Teach your counselee about flesh strategies, using *Strategies to Meet Unmet Needs.* (See diagram 3.)
6. Make sure your counselee understands the struggle involved in making changes, and what it means to *crucify the flesh* (diagrams 7 and 8). *P 105 & 106*
7. Work with your counselee to understand the process of forgiveness and acceptance.
8. Reinforce positive, Scripture-based cognitive messages that enhance healing.
9. Assign participation in recreational activities (sunlight and exercise, being with people).
10. Memorize appropriate Scriptures and assign daily meditation of selected Psalms. Encourage journaling.

HOMEWORK

1. Give your counselee a copy of *Who am I?* and *Why did God Make Me?* to reflect on the truth of his identity as a spiritual person.

2. Give your counselee a copy of *Emotional Responses to Unmet Needs* and ask him to identify his *unreachable goals*.

3. Assign your counselee to read *Feelings, What Good are They?* to determine what is the *unreachable goal*.

4. Assign your counselee to read "The Healthiness of Depression" by Scott Peck in *A Road Less Traveled* to understand the nature of depression, and to identify what needs to change.

5. Give your counselee a copy of *Strategies to Meet Unmet Needs* (diagram 3) and ask him to identify his own flesh strategies.

6. Give your counselee articles on forgiveness.

7. Assign your counselee to reflect on, study, and memorize pertinent Scriptures.

EXAMPLE OF A STRATEGIC TREATMENT PLAN FOR DEPRESSION

Case Scenario: Cindy

1. Engaging

Build Rapport; Set Boundaries; Identify Reason for Counseling

Cindy, age 39, sought counseling for her depression which had become increasingly more severe in the last few years. Although Cindy had been in psychotherapy for three years until about five months ago, she said she had learned little about why she was depressed: her therapist had referred her to a psychiatrist who prescribed anti-depressants. When I asked her why she had quit counseling with her therapist, she explained it had not really helped very much. [Of course I thought it was significant that she had stayed in therapy so long when by her own admission, it was not helping. Over the years I have found that many counselees continue in counseling that is ineffective because they assume that if it is not effective, it must be their fault—rather than assuming the counselor's approach is ineffective!] I asked Cindy what was the catalyst for her call to me. She said she heard about me from a friend and wanted to see if Biblical counseling might help. I could tell that Cindy was leery of committing to a new counselor, so I assured Cindy that I could help her and that it was NOT going to take three years to discover the cause of her depression, that we would probably meet for three or four sessions and then decide how to continue after that.

Relevant History

Cindy had been married for 12 years—she said her husband was a responsible man but was not meeting her deep emotional needs. It was simply that he did not seem to engage her deeply when she needed to talk—he was glued to the sports channel on TV most of the time. It was apparent to her he did not care about her problems. Cindy wondered if she had married the wrong person—she had not dated too many men and at 27 had decided she better accept her husband's proposal as she might not have another opportunity.

Cindy had three children—a boy and two girls—all in grade school. They were good children, that is, no one had any unusual problem, but Cindy admitted that she had little joy in being a mother. She was plagued with guilt that she was not emotionally connected to them as she should be. As I probed a little further into her history, Cindy explained that her own mother and father had divorced when she was in grade school. Both of her parents were absorbed in their own problems and did not show much interest in Cindy or her sister. She felt very disconnected from them even to this day.

I inquired of her church and social life. Cindy was involved in a women's Bible study, but was not deeply connected to anyone there. I asked about her spiritual life: When was she born again? Did she have a daily prayer or study time? Not surprisingly, Cindy confessed feeling guilty about her lack of hunger for God. When she approached God in prayer, she explained, "it was like the lights were on, but nobody was home!"

2. Diagnosis (see page 183)

3. Setting Goals

Cindy and I agreed to the following goals:

1) We would understand the source of depressed feelings and identify her *unreachable goals* at root of her depression.
2) We would identify what God wants to change in order to move beyond depression to spiritual and emotional healthiness to accept her circumstances, past and present, in the context of GOD's sovereignty.

4. Replacing Wrong Thinking with Biblical Thinking

1) I taught Cindy about depression, using *Understanding Emotional Reactions to Unmet Needs*. We identified Cindy's unreachable goals and unmet expectations.
2) I helped Cindy to see the negative messages she was still believing about herself and taught her about her "new" identity in Christ, no longer a *son of [Adam]* but a *son of God*, no longer *conformed to this world* but *transformed*.
3) I taught Cindy about fleshly strategies and the struggle involved in making changes, and what it would mean to crucify her flesh (diagrams 7 and 8).

HOMEWORK

1) I assigned Cindy to read: *Who Am I?* and *Why did God Make Me?* and *Feelings, What Good Are They?*   P77
2) I gave Cindy a copy of *Strategies to Meet Unmet Needs* (diagram 3) and asked her to identify her own flesh strategies.
3) I gave Cindy a copy of *Emotional Responses to Unmet Needs* and ask her to identify her *unreachable goals*.

4) I assigned Cindy to read articles on forgiveness in order to let go of unmet expectations and goal-oriented behaviors and move toward forgiveness.

5) I assigned Cindy to read a chapter called "The Healthiness of Depression" from Scott Peck's book *The Road Less Traveled*. Note: even though this is not a Christian book, the short chapter provides an insightful explanation of depression that it is a signal that "something needs to change" in order for the person to be relieved of his depression. This theme is very compatible with the Biblical principle of *putting off the old self*.

Diagnosis for Cindy	
Step One **Is Cindy feeling most deficient in:** *Belonging?* *Love and Acceptance?* *Feeling that she matters?*	It is very apparent in listening to Cindy's story, that she feels a lack of "belonging" (connectedness) to her husband and to her children. It is not difficult to see the correlation between her lack of belonging to her parents and an exaggerated need to belong to her husband and children.
Step Two Identify Problem Feelings	Cindy is depressed. Her depression did not really show itself until she had been married for a few years and had her second child.
Step Three Identify Problem Behaviors	Cindy does "everything" she is supposed to do to be a good wife and mother, but has little joy in doing it. However, she admits that she withdraws from her husband and is often impatient with her children.
Step Four Identify Problem Thinking	From her feeling of disconnectedness, Cindy "fantasized" as a child about growing up and getting married, and living a perfect life. She told herself she would feel happy when she had a husband and children.

Conclusion: Subconsciously, Cindy was expecting to "feel" this sense of belonging when she got married. No one could have filled this void. But Cindy was unaware that her depression was telling her that she had an unreachable goal, unreasonable expectations that she would find in her husband and children someone who could fill that void and make her feel that she belonged. With each child and each passing year, the goal was getting more and more unreachable.

Questions and Answers about Strategic Biblical Counseling

Question:

Dr. Burts, you say that our counselees must be changed from the "inside out," that they cannot truly change until their minds have been enlightened or renewed. How do I proceed if my counselee says he already "knows" the truth but his behavior says otherwise?

Answer:

The Apostle Paul must have had this problem too because in his prayers he asks God to give revelation knowledge to the believers at Ephesus, Philippi, and Colossi. The answer to your question is: "PRAY!" First, pray with and for your counselee that he or she will comprehend and apprehend these life changing truths. Second, pray that God will give you wisdom and insight to teach and impart these truths to your counselee. Use diagrams that illustrate the truth. Have your counselee read about these truths, study them, meditate upon them, and memorize them. Then pray some more, and proceed with your mutually agreed upon goals. Revelation will come in God's time.

> *Note: Over the years I have had many occasions when I labored to impart a particular truth to my counselee with apparent failure. Then one day, he comes in to my office and tells me that he heard a sermon or read a book and now he has understood a particular truth for the first time. He credits the preacher or author with having enlightened him. He does not know that 1) I have been teaching this truth to him for weeks, and 2) the Holy Spirit—not the teacher—revealed this truth to him. I do not care when or where my counselees come into a revelation of the truth. It is not a matter of who gets the credit! We must remember it is the Holy Spirit's role to impart truth.*

Question:

Dr. Burts, you said that Strategic Biblical Counseling is "brief." How will we help people who have chronic problems and need long term support?

Answer:

The church is the ideal environment for meeting the needs of people who have a need for ongoing support. Small fellowship groups, recovery groups, or other accountability groups are important to the growth process of individuals in our congregations. If your church is not large enough to have such support groups, do not be afraid to avail yourself of these resources in other churches. Also, there are many "Para-local church" organizations that offer support services.

Question:

Where does forgiveness fit into Strategic Biblical Counseling?

Answer:

Forgiveness is a normal part of "letting go" of expectations—of others and of your self. This is part of the needs-based paradigm where counselees realize they have been expecting others to meet their needs. Please note that in the "Setting Goals" section of the Strategic Treatment Plan, I have suggested that forgiving others is a short term goal. This is especially true of people who are angry because of others' expectations of them or for disappointments in others and/or offenses against them. There are so many resources on the subject of "forgiveness," I have not seen any reason to address this subject in any depth.

Question:

Dr. Burts, with respect to support groups, what is your opinion about Alcoholics Anonymous (AA) or Christian 12-step programs?

Answer:

Over the years, I have counseled many people who have been involved in AA. Some of them met other Christians in AA and were able to fellowship with them. Some actually were brought to Christ through other members in AA. AA and other such support groups can be an excellent supplementary support for counselees struggling with severe addictive behavior. However, I must stress the word "supplementary" because

I have seen people replace the church with AA. This should never be. AA may be used as a supplement to a counselee's spiritual growth through sound Bible teaching, Bible study and fellowship with healthy believers.

> *Note: I will not counsel a person who has an active addiction (still substance abusing) unless he or she is in a support or accountability group. Such persons who are still struggling are not good candidates for one-on-one counseling until they have a larger network of support. Seeing a counselor once a week is simply not enough. Also, I do not want to 'make it easy' for such persons to avoid the group dynamics of a support group: this is part of the dysfunction that underlies the addictive behavior.*

Question:

The Strategic Biblical Counseling model assumes counselees have deficits in their needs. Does this model fit for counselees with "normal-life" problems such as a divorce, death of spouse/parent/child, a loss of a job, a serious accident, a terminal illness?

Answer:

The "needs-based" approach of Strategic Biblical Counseling works in any situation. When someone has experienced any loss in his or her life, he or she will be angry or depressed as a normal part of "grieving." Remember, our definition of "anger" is a "blocked goal" and our definition of "depression" is an "unreachable goal." [Refer to chapter five, "What is Wrong with Me" and chapter nine, "Feelings, What Good are They?"] Whether the counselee has lost a family member, a job, or his health, he will benefit from Strategic Biblical Counseling. His

or her goal-oriented behaviors will have to change because
the way he or she used to meet that need is no longer possible.

> Note: Many people who are going through a separation or
> divorce are either angry or depressed, or both. They are expe-
> riencing a very real loss. They are grieving. Their goal of a
> good marriage, an intact family, or "growing old together"
> has become unreachable. The final stage of grief is "accep-
> tance." My objective in counseling such persons is to help them
> move toward accepting a situation over which they have no
> control, trusting God to protect and provide for their needs.
> In most cases, the counselee needs to re-define his or her life.
> Who better than a Biblical counselor to help such persons see
> themselves from a spiritual and eternal perspective?

Question:

How does the Strategic Biblical Counseling model work for
marriage counseling?

Answer:

It is my opinion that traditional marriage counseling (couple
therapy) does not work for most couples. When marriage
partners are deeply conflicted and angry at one another, they
use the counseling session to vent at each other and validate
themselves. This is not progressive—it is regressive. Therefore, I have found it more effective to separate the partners
and conduct individual counseling sessions where each partner sets goals for him/herself and is accountable to the counselor for his or her own changes. Even then the partners may
want to use the counseling session venting about their spouse.
When this happens, I remind the counselee that the goal of

our counseling is not to change his/her spouse but to focus on what God wants to change in "me."

> *Note: I have found a booklet written by Nancy Missler (from Koinonia House), "Why Should I be the First to Change?" very helpful reading for women who are angry or depressed because their husbands are not meeting their needs. I think it goes without saying, but I will say so anyway, in lay counseling situations, women should be counseled by women and men by men. Paul says the* "older women should teach the younger women how to love their husbands and children."
>
> (Titus 2:3–4)

Question:

How would I know if my counselee is psychotic? When would I refer a counselee to a psychiatrist or a psychotherapist?

Answer:

A psychotic person's perception of reality is distorted. Thus they may have hallucinations, be paranoid or delusional. They have disorganized thinking. Because Strategic Biblical Counseling is so cognitively oriented, it is less effective when people have disordered or scattered thinking. These persons need special ministry. In some cases, these persons should be referred for psychiatric evaluations. There are medical remedies—prescription drugs—that can help reduce some of the psychotic person's symptoms. If a psychotic person responds well to medication, he may be able to respond to the cognitive approach of Strategic Biblical Counseling.

Question:

Dr. Burts, do you believe antidepressants or other prescription drugs are appropriate for a Christian? When would I refer a depressed person to a medical doctor for evaluation?

Answer:

Depression is a complicated "issue." There are so many factors relating to depression: circumstance, physical health, genetics, diet, stress, environment, etc. Also an increasing number of people are being diagnosed with bipolar disorder (manic-depressive illness). With bi-polar disorder and major depression, medications are prescribed. Unfortunately, the whole arena of pharmacology is somewhat experimental. For depression, anti-depressants may be effective in increasing low serotonin levels. For bipolar disorder, mood stabilizers are prescribed. I do not believe it is wrong for people to use prescription drugs if the symptoms (of the depression or mania) are overwhelming. Many people have been helped. The real question is: "Can Strategic Biblical Counseling help these people?" The answer is yes. Even people struggling with depression can benefit from the needs-based, cognitive approach of Strategic Biblical Counseling.

Question:

Dr. Burts, in the chapter "What is a Biblical Counselor," you refer to the ministry of burden bearing. In a church environment, how does the lay Biblical counselor maintain objectivity and avoid creating a dependent relationship?

Answer:

Objectivity may be affected because of interactions the counselor may have with that person in church life. However, to protect the one-on-one counseling session from too much familiarity, lay Biblical counselors should not counsel a person with whom they have a personal, ongoing relationship. We need to distinguish the ministry of mentoring and discipleship from the ministry of counseling.

Question:

How does the lay Biblical counselor maintain confidentiality in a church setting if the pastor(s) want to know about the person's problems and progress?

Answer:

Whenever I have helped to establish a lay counseling ministry in a church, I have insisted that there be a "zero tolerance" policy with respect to confidentiality. The first time there is any indication a counselor has broken confidentiality, he or she is dismissed from the counseling team. However, the counselee should sign a release form acknowledging that the lay counselor may share the counselee's issues with their pastor, as appropriate. Remember, lay Biblical counselors are an extension of pastoral care.

Question:

How does a counselor decide what kinds of people he can best help?

Answer:

There is a truism that you cannot take anyone further than you have been yourself. It is my conviction that unlike secular therapists, Biblical counselors should not counsel "issues" that are unresolved in their own lives. There is a higher standard because of the spiritual responsibility: Biblical counselors should meet the standards of a deacon, as prescribed in Paul's letter to Timothy. They should be above reproach. For example, a woman who is unhappy in her marriage should not be counseling other women who are unhappy in their marriages. Or a man who is still struggling with pornography will not be able to help others who are struggling.

Question:

Dr. Burts, you say in the chapter "What is Biblical Counseling?" that Biblical counselors operate with "spiritual authority," yet you have not spoken much about spiritual warfare in your book. What does a Biblical counselor do if he discerns a person has demonic strongholds?

Answer:

To address the subject of spiritual warfare would require a separate book. I recommend the Biblical counselor read *Handbook for Spiritual Warfare*, by Dr. Ed Murphy (available through Nelson Publishers).

Question:

Some suffering is legitimate. Some is a consequence of our own sins. Some is caused by others when we are the innocent victim. How does one help people who suffer chronically?

Answer:

This topic is also too huge to cover in brevity. So let me recommend *Don't Waste Your Sorrows* by Paul Bilheimer, *When
God Weeps* by Joni Eareckson Tada, and *Pain, Perplexity &
Promotion: A Prophetic Interpretation of the Book of Job*, by Bob
Sorge, as a few of my favorites. However, there are many books
and resource materials available to the Biblical counselor on
this important subject.

Question:

I have heard that child abuse is required to be reported to
police or to child protection agencies. Are pastors and lay
Biblical counselors exempt from this requirement? Are there
other things, like domestic abuse, elder abuse that are mandatory reporting issues?

Answer:

All 50 states have passed some form of a mandatory child abuse
and neglect reporting law in order to qualify for funding under
the Child Abuse Prevention and Treatment Act, 42 U.S.C. 5101.
Some states provide an exemption for clergy who receive information in the context of a sacred communication or confession. The clergy/penitent exception, however, is strictly defined
and will not apply if a clergyman is acting in another role, i.e. a
health practitioner. Therefore, lay Biblical counselors are not
exempt and must report child abuse. Any reporting should always be done by way of the pastor. Any other issues regarding
the care and protection of people should be discussed with the
pastor or elders. To know if there are any other mandatory
reporting requirements for mental health practitioners in your
state, check with local social service authorities.

To order additional copies of

STRATEGIC BIBLICAL COUNSELING

Have your credit card ready and call:

1-877-421-READ (7323)

or please visit our web site at
www.pleasantword.com

Also available at:
www.amazon.com
and
www.barnesandnoble.com

Printed in the United States
66051LVS00001B/73-80

9 781414 103440